What people said about C

'Inspirational. Original. Quirky. Amusing. Cau
water dreams come true – and do it on a budge
cartoon-illustrated handbook.'
Paul Gelder, Editor, Yachting Monthly

'A chucklingly amusing account of cruising in
experienced it all first-hand. This is an easy read to dip into as your fancy takes you and
had me giggling and nodding in agreement with almost every page. The author's entertaining anecdotes are delightfully illustrated by his own hand, which adds a further dimension
to this hilarious little book.'
Duncan Kent, Editor, Sailing Today

'This is a funny book that will keep you up all night reading it. As Bob says, "Buy a copy,
I need the money."'
Latitudes and Attitudes magazine, USA

'...a delightful and ironic look at the cruising life... its cartoon illustrations brings out the
humour of living aboard... pokes fun at every angle of the cruising life.'
Sail magazine, USA

'It is beautifully written and brilliantly observed with great cartoons. Hilarious from start
to finish... and you get the added bonus of very funny cartoons.'
Duncan Wells

'I wanted to let you know that we have the copy with us on board as we sail through the
Med and think it is great.'
Emily Jallat, Yacht Wollombi II

'I can't wait for 'Bang on the nose' to be born... 'On the nose' was fantastic!
Excellent Christmas present for any age...'
Robin Ramdeen, Trinidad

'We just wanted to let you know how much we enjoyed your book... ?!!! The illustrations
were a book in themselves. We can't tell you how much we giggled and chuckled our way
through them.'
Sue Dockrell

'I thought it was fantastic, very funny, and the illustrations were brilliant too... wonderful,
a great read... I shall look forward to reading your further adventures.'
Fiona Ryan

'I was given your book 'On the Nose' for Christmas, and haven't had such a good laugh
for ages, it brought back a lot of memories. Your chapter on anchoring made me howl with
laughter.... thank you.'
Ann Goulden

On the nose

A song for Mediterranean yachties (in the key of A, transposed from E#)

A   E
The wife and I went cruising in the blue Aegean Sea
 E   A
We practised all our sail trim, yes, both the wife and me
  A7   D
We looked forward to some crackin' sails but it was not to be
    A   E   A
Because the Mediterranean wind is on the nose

Chorus
A   E
On the nose, on the nose
A   E
The blasted wind is slap bang on the nose
 A   A7
We don't know where it comes from
 D
But we all know where it goes
    A   E   A
Because the Mediterranean wind is on the nose

We tried to get to Istanbul in the dreaded Meltemi
We tried it twice and then the wife said 'That's enough for me'
The current from the Dardanelles was awfully strong you see
And the Mediterranean wind is on the nose

Chorus

There's the Mistral and the Scirocco and the Bora and the Gregale
and the Meltemi and the Tramontana and the Etesian and the Khamsin
and the Levanter and the Ghibli and the Libeccio and the Leveche
and the Poniente to name but three or four *(deep breath)*
They named one for every compass point then they named a shedload more
We don't care where they come from 'cause we all know where they goes
Because the Mediterranean wind is on the nose

Chorus

If you can think up any more verses, email me. I'll put them in the next book.

A very queer thing is the wind,
I don't know how it beginn'd,
But ev'ryone knows where it goes,
It is wind, and it blows on the nose.

Apologies to John Masefield

Bang on the nose

written and illustrated by
Bob Cooper

NOSETHEON BOOKS

© Bob Cooper 2010

Published by

Nosetheon Books, Ship to Shore, P O Box 400, Winchester, SO22 4RY
nosetheon@yahoo.co.uk

UK ISBN 978-0-9559256-1-0

Illustrations: Bob Cooper
Copy-editing: Andrew Morley
Design and typesetting: Bob Cooper
Image scanning and digitising: Liz Cooper
Printed in China, on behalf of MBC Print

Contents

The characters in this book are all real. Only the names have been changed to protect the guilty. Then again some have been left so as to cause maximum embarrassment. If you think you've found yourself in this book, I can only apologise. But don't worry because this isn't the real world; it's Cartoonland. And a word for the experienced cruiser reading this book. I've written it for a wide audience so please bear with me and skip all the explanations to things that you'll already know more about than I do. Go and have a coffee or something then come back to the next cartoon.

For Eric and Dot

Ship's log: stardate 031006

Our tiny craft, a miniscule speck of life in the enveloping darkness, glided almost silently along the boundary layer of the two fluids covering the rocky surface of the planet. Above us countless coldly glittering stars; an equal infinity of swirls and points of light swept around and below us. Standing at the controls, my eyelids drooped. I was almost lulled into that delicious state of half-waking half-dreaming by the steady deep thrumming of the oleoinfusion drive beneath my feet.

Flash! I was jolted awake by a blinding white light searing into the cockpit. Turning to look directly at the blazing circle of light energy that was its source, I made out dim shadowy figures standing next to it. Aliens! Our first contact with sentient beings since the start of our seemingly endless odyssey from Sira Cusa Base. Would they be friendly? My heart thumping wildly, I slowly raised a hand and tentatively waved a greeting. I thought I saw a movement in response.

Then just as suddenly the light snapped out, and I heard the deep throb of the alien craft's engines turn to a snarling roar as it powered away into the blackness. With shaking hands I returned to the controls and tried to concentrate on steering our little vessel. Aliens, I thought, our first contact. But what if that was a scout ship, a welcoming party from the mother ship somewhere ahead in the inky darkness? What sort of strange and unknown craft were we speeding toward? It might be a huge battle cruiser, the size of a small city maybe, and built to withstand centuries of attack, siege and warfare. What would such a battle-scarred behemoth make of us?

Ahead, I could just make out faint lights that didn't seem to be stars; they were slowly growing in intensity, becoming steadier and more focused. The darkness too was giving way gently to a gradually strengthening hint of light. Dawn. A dark menacing presence was looming up behind the lights, growing in size and clarity. I looked ahead, mesmerised by the huge blocky shape that was slowly coming into view. As the light grew, I could begin to make out features on its surface: domes, towers (antennae?) and spikes (were they guns?), encrusted the fortress-like structure. And with the light came colour. The entire edifice was one colour, the dusty buff of ancient stones.

I was stirred from my reveries as my companion climbed up into the cockpit. She stood, stretched, yawned, turned and looked ahead.

And gasped in amazement.

1

'Blimey! It's the Millennium Falcon, only in stone!'

'Nice one, Princess Leia, but that's Valletta. Been a really good night sail, lots of phosphorescence in the water. Dolphins too. The Coast Guard checked us out half an hour ago, and if we get our skates on we'll be tied up in Msida Creek just in time for a Full English Breakfast, baked beans, fried bread, the lot. This is Malta!'

Well, OK, Valletta looked like a battle-scarred intergalactic cruiser to *us* anyway. It's an appropriate analogy given Malta's history of bangs, battles and bombs. It's one reason why I called this book *Bang on the nose*. Of course we never meant to go to Malta. That's where the Royal Navy was, wasn't it? It's going to be all badly-cooked British grub, cheap fags and Daily Express readers, isn't it? But dusty, trafficky, bustling Malta, grew on us. We explored the island, did all our boat jobs, met the delightful Maltesers, renewed old friendships, found new ones, and dined, danced and drank our way through the whole winter. I also broke my collarbone and started to write *On the nose*. So thanks to Malta for that. I'm going to write quite a bit about it in a while but don't worry. It's definitely worth it.

Le grand cul-de-sac

But to backtrack, what were we doing in Malta anyway? Well, eighteen months previously Liz and I had set off from Scotland in our Warrior 35 sailing boat, Yanina of Bosham. We crossed the Bay of Biscay, headed down the Atlantic coast of Spain and Portugal, turned left at Cape St Vincent and entered the Med. After a winter in a Spanish marina (entertaining), we sailed east to the Balearics (delightful), Sardinia (they'll nick your dinghy), Corsica (very rugged), Italy's west coast and Sicily. If you want to read all about it, buy my first book *On the nose: a sideways look at cruising and living aboard in the western Mediterranean.* You can buy it at www.bookharbour.com, order it from a bookshop, or if you're skint the library will get it for you.

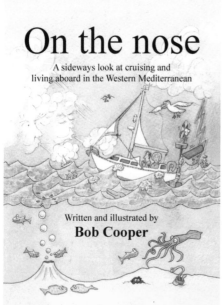

On the nose has so far achieved what I'd call modest success, and everyone has said nice things about it, for which thank you one and all. In fact I must be nearly famous because the other day when I was manoeuvring Yanina a bit too close to a big shiny BFO motor yacht, the owner waved his peaked cap at me and shouted over and called me a cult. At least that's what it sounded like - I couldn't quite hear above the engine noise.

This book* - the book you're holding in your grubby sweaty hands (look, you could at least buy it now you've got thumbprints all over it; the shopkeeper's fed up with you coming in every day to read it, and no dog-eared pages, please. One day somebody will buy this book on Amazon New and Used for £00.01plus P & P £9.98, and they'll want a decent copy) - this book follows on from *On the nose*, and will take us from Malta to Greece, to Turkey, and back again.

As I write, Yanina is now in the Caribbean, on the hard (always worries me, that phrase) in Grenada, hoping to escape the next hurricane. Yes, we finally got out of the Med. But it took us four years…

*To those of you who were desperately looking for a book called *Right on the nose*, as I described it in *On the nose*, I apologise. Must be frustrating when the author tells you one thing then does another. But you have to admit it's a better title.

… because once you're in, it's not that easy to escape. Before they cut the canal at Suez, the Strait of Gibraltar was the only way in or out and the Med was one big cul-de-sac*. In effect it still is, and within it you'll find hundreds of little cul-de-sacs full of lots of yachties hanging around, enjoying the sun and the lifestyle, and just not wanting to leave.

Of course you can leave through the Suez Canal, but what a palaver that is. You pay a fortune in fees and bribes just to get through it, then just as you're beginning to enjoy the Red Sea, you get shot at or kidnapped by pirates on the way to the Indian Ocean. And once you're past that little duck shoot you say to yourself: 'Well, well, well. I'm out of the Med. I suppose I may as well go round the world now,' and that's when you realise that you're going the wrong way, against the prevailing winds, and you'll have a real job on your hands to get through all the Pacific archipelagos and up to Panama, through t'cut to the Caribbean, and into the teeth of the Atlantic Trade Winds and all the big steep horrible waves that the Trades have piled up ready for you off the coast of Colombia. So not the route most sailors will choose, although a few perverse thrill-seekers do go that way every year.

You can try to escape by going through the Dardanelles and up past Istanbul into the Black Sea. OK, you're out of the Med but you're into another arse-of-ze-bag, and it's full of Bulgarians and friends of Borat.

And it's not just that it's comfy, warm and cheap to live in that keeps yachties in the Med; when you get back to the Straits of Gibraltar, you face a strong east-setting current and a complicated set of tidal streams, making escape so tricky that people have written entire books about how to sail through. If the Med were a Black Hole, the Straits would be the event horizon.

So what the heck? Why not relax and enjoy it? We'll start with Malta.

*or, translated directly from the French vernacular: Arse-of-ze-bag

5

Round the block a few times

There *are* bits of green on Malta (even more on Gozo, its country cousin) but by and large it's the same dusty stone colour as Valletta, because most of it's jam-packed with buildings. All, apart from the recent rash of new hotels, are constructed from the same identical limestone blocks, probably still measured in cubits, that have been quarried from the land itself for millennia. The island is stone. The buildings are stone. The buildings are the island. It's a giant stone Lego kit!

Malta parks itself like an ancient dusty battle-worn tank on a rocky mini-roundabout bang in the middle of the crossroads between the Eastern and Western Med. For so long fought over, besieged, and desperately defended, it's a small but fiercely proud outpost of Christianity thumbing its nose at the Muslim Maghreb to the south. Although their language is based on Arabic, the Maltese are fiercely Catholic, and would say proudly and loudly that their tongue is simply Maltese.

This strong religious loyalty combined with an island siege mentality engenders a deep reluctance to depart from tradition. Not only in the buildings. The luzzu, the traditional wooden boat of Malta and built like an ancient Roman galley, bears a local version of the Eye of Horus on its steep bow. And what a paint job. Each luzzu is a small floating explosion of intense colour, as if to compensate for the monochrome of the surrounding buildings.

Here's a Christmas card I did of Santa doing his deliveries by luzzu, much more practical than a sleigh.

But not all the boats in Malta's creeks are shaped like floating bananas with beady eyes. Some local naval architects have adopted a more minimal and modernist approach to boat-building and hieroglyphics.

And tradition hasn't stopped the resourceful, adaptable Maltese from learning how to repair anything that floats. The Royal Navy was there for so long that local craftsmen could soon deal with anything the Navy threw at them, so now Malta is one of the best places in the Med to have just about anything done to your boat. The Knights of St John were sailors; when they arrived they settled in Birgu in Grand Harbour, rather than the ancient capital of Mdina up the hill. I'm sure they got on better with the local Practical Luzzu Owners than with the posh nobs up in Mdina.

So all in all there's a long and ancient tradition on the island of not just messing about in boats, but building, maintaining and repairing them too.

Even so, when you get your topsides painted in Malta just be careful.

On the buses

Get the local bus and you'll think you're in a working transport museum. Leylands, Scammells, AECs and Bedfords, they were imported from Britain in the 50s. Each has a home-made shrine above the driver's seat, and passengers often cross themselves before they set off on what after all may be a trip to eternity, given the devil-may-care approach of the driver. Santa didn't care either.

Religion and relics: one off the wrist

It all started when St Paul got shipwrecked in Malta. As a reward for being rescued he convinced the Maltese to stop worshipping limestone blocks and to follow Jesus instead, and they still have a memento of the occasion. Tony Bennett may have left his heart in San Francisco but St Paul left his wrist bone in Valletta, mounted in a golden forearm and hand and placed on display in St Paul's Shipwreck Church.

It's a popular Mediterranean pastime, dismembering your favourite saint and displaying the leftovers. It certainly pulls in the tourists today, and looking back, just think what profitable marketing opportunities the medieval trade in bone fragments must have offered. No DNA, no provenance, just the word of an unscrupulous cleric with a sack of sheep's ribs round the back of the cloisters.

And then there's the Prepuce of Our Lord, originally given to Charlemagne, King of the Franks and son of Pippin the Short, by an angel. Allegedly. It was paraded annually in Calcata, near Rome, until 1983 when it was stolen. It had been kept in a shoe box at the back of a priest's wardrobe. Good job the Maltese didn't get hold of it - I know just how they'd display it.

But leaving foreskins aside (as all who had the op must do), I think Paul must have been very persuasive in Malta. If you think of the Church as a big multi-national corporation whose celestial CEO had sent his terrestrial Sales Director out to open up lucrative new markets, only to arrange a storm that very nearly took him back to the Pearly Gates, how do you sell that to the natives?

'Look, Maltesers, I know it was the Boss's will to wreck my ship here, thus delaying my sales campaign by several years, but really it was all for the best, basically because you don't argue with Him. So if you all sign up to this Holy Moses ten-point life insurance plan, I won't ask Him to send you to eternal hellfire and damnation.' Damn good sales technique, I say.

← Golden hand of St Paul as it appeared above the waves just before his rescue

← Wristbone of St Paul

← Golden arm of St Paul

← Rolled-up sleeve of St Paul

← The snake that bit St P on the wrist with no effect whatsoever

WRISTBONE OF ST PAUL

St Paul's statue and his wrist bone are given an airing every February in the streets of Valletta, with a mighty wailing and a gnashing of teeth. But sometimes the religious fervour diminishes and the Maltese good humour and sense of fun come smiling through. I saw these two nuns debating whether they might, just might, have a go on the bouncy castle.

Bangs, battles and bombs

When two Maltese have a conversation, it's like hearing firecrackers going off. It seems an invitation to a punch-up, but it's not. The Maltese are just up front about what they say and think. And it's there in the signs and slogans you see everywhere, with religion usually the subject. On buses you'll see *Destination Darkness*, or *Jesus is the lover of my soul*, or perhaps the more practical *Don't follow me, I'm lost too*. Car owners share more secular thoughts with you: *Back off unless you have tits*, *Keep your distance, your wife or daughter may be a passenger*, or the brisk and to the point *F#*k your opinions*. Public signs display this directness too. In the Nazzjonal Swimming Pool you'll see *Don't pee in our pool, we don't swim in your toilet*.

This upfrontedness must have been forged in Malta's long and bloody history of warfare and siege. The best known siege took place in 1565, where 40,000 Turks were defeated by a few hundred Knights of St John, some Spanish soldiers and the Maltese themselves. Suleiman the Magnificent was not pleased. In 1797 Bonaparte did better, and immediately set about melting down anything made out of precious metal and carting it off to Paris. Three years later, having eaten all the frogs and snails on the island and finding Maltese rabbit stew every single day quite unendurable, the French had gone.

And who picked up the pieces? The British Navy of course! They stayed there for about 165 years, eventually co-hosting Malta's other great Siege, with that wonderful wacky wartime double act, Adolf and Benito.

So today Malta's past is celebrated with wartime relics and explosions. In the National War Museum you can see 'Faith', one of the six Gloster Gladiators which held off the Italian Air Force, forcing them to drop their bombs into the sea. Can't help thinking there was a bit of sympathy for Malta there on the part of the bomb aimers. Probably all Sicilian lads. No sympathy from the Luftwaffe though, Malta suffered 3000 bombing raids in two years, and got hammered so much that they created their very own 'Maltese rubble' camouflage as seen in the War Museum. They also got the George Cross which appears on their flag - not the Maltese Cross as you'd expect.

There are drill re-enactments where they do scary things like shooting wads of paper from small cannons. You can indulge in a bit of pyrotechnification at the spectacular annual international fireworks competition. Or see the occasional firing of the enormous, totally under-used and really quite Art Deco 10-metre long 100-ton gun on Fort Rinella.

It's as if the Maltese find it all too quiet for them in peacetime and they have to create a few bangs to make up for it.

Did you know? To make a Maltese cross you poke him in the eye, but to make a Maltese flag, you have to chase him round the harbour.

11

A Maltese physical type

So what did all these Maltese hard cases that fought the Turks, the French, the Italians and the Germans look like? According to Ernle Bradford in *The Great Siege: Malta 1565,* 'Alongside (the Knights of St John) stood the dark, short-legged, barrel-chested men of Malta. A sturdy race of islanders, descendants perhaps of the Phoenicians, they proved... that they could endure almost unbelievable hardships.' I read this and realised that I was meeting their descendants everywhere.

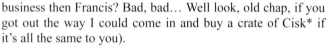

People like Francis Portelli, or maybe it was his shop assistant, who stood all day in the doorway of his liquor emporium, on the lookout for likely customers. But any would-be customer had to think twice about forcing their way into the shop (How's business then Francis? Bad, bad... Well look, old chap, if you got out the way I could come in and buy a crate of Cisk* if it's all the same to you).

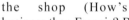

Did the Maltese foot soldiers on the ramparts of the battlements of Fort St Angelo in 1565 stand in that same way, looking left and right, on the lookout for likely Turkish invaders? Probably.

Then there was the girl that my friend Nige, never one to mince words, christened The Fat Prostitute. She would smile, stroke her hair and charmingly propositioning any passing male pedestrian. Her street was the short cut between the marina and all the chandlery shops where yachties spent what few euros remained to them after purchasing all those crates of Cisk from portly Francis Portelli. She became part of the directions given to any new arrival: 'Turn right after The Fat Prostitute and Gauci Borda's third on the left. You can't miss it.'

But you could imagine her hurling the odd bucket of boiling pitch over the battlements. Probably got the Turks quite excited.

---

* Cisk (pronounced 'Chisk') is Malta's very own lager. Probably the best lager on the island

Or what about Tony who ran the small but perfectly-formed Slipway Lounge Bar down by the waterfront in Msida. Or his brother who was the Maltese Eurovision Song Contest entry for 1970-something, wearing what looked suspiciously like a big black afro wig. Tony'll show you the video if you ask nicely.

Tony's brother's wig apart, this lot are the spitting image of those peasant soldiers who, on the orders of Grand Master de la Vallette, hacked the heads off the Turkish captives and used them as cannonballs.

Don't mess with a Malteser. The short bald ones are the worst. See the resemblance? Over four centuries too.

Testaferrata Street

Walk past Tony's Slipway Lounge bar, up the hill on the northern side of Msida Creek and you'd get to Testaferrata Street*, leading downhill to the chandlery shops. Testaferrata Street was where all the working girls were.

Just opposite the supermarket on the first floor above the Skoda dealers (this is Malta) that had a butcher that was a dead ringer for the young Rodney Bewes, there on the street were the working girls, some with lovely smiles, some with faces like carved granite (or do I mean Maltese limestone). They'd sit in doorways or click around on high heels holding mobile phones to their heads, or lean into car windows, doing business. It's a living.

I wonder if they were there in 1565? I could just picture one of them helping the odd Knight of St John out of his codpiece for a bit of pre-siege executive relaxation before the Turks arrived.

* Testaferrata means either 'iron head' or 'iron testicles'. You decide. I couldn't possibly comment.

Maltese pets

The gentler side of the Maltese character can most easily be seen in their attitude to their pets. As a small island, Malta has an appropriately small dog - the Maltese Pocket Dog, or Teacup Dog. You'll see big burly blokes cuddling one of these tiny shivering canines. Why you would want to put a dog in a teacup or your pocket is something the Maltese know best - I suppose it saves on a collar and lead, and also the embarrassment of walking along the Maltese pavements with those vulgar British tourists shouting 'Look! A rat on a piece of string' at you.

And what about that young goat walking nonchalantly along the pavement on a lead past Francis Portelli's shop three pages ago looking as if it popped along the high street with its owner for a paper every morning of the week. Which it probably did. Maybe it ate yesterday's papers. Goats do that.

And then just over the bridge to Manoel Island and the boatyard, someone has built Duck Village, a dotty collection of wooden boxes and ramps housing a small collective noun of ducks.

One minute the Maltese are ripping the heads off visiting Turks; the next they're putting dogs in their pockets or building little sheltered housing complexes for the ducks.

But what of our fellow yachties in Msida Creek? Ian and Sue on their beautiful big old Swan had been at Almerimar with us in our first winter, but we didn't get to know them until we met in Malta. Whatever Ian may tell you about his ailments which he monitors carefully, he's a bon viveur and a party animal. He and Sue love dancing, and within minutes of telling you about his high blood pressure they'll be boogie-ing away until four in the morning. So I did this cartoon for them. And where in Malta did they boogie the night away?

IAN DECIDED TO GIVE HIS NEW
BLOOD PRESSURE MONITOR A
THOROUGHLY GOOD WORKOUT......

The Black Pearl

The Black Pearl, that's where. She was a 100 year-old wooden three-master, once owned by Errol Flynn. Sunk twice, she was raised from the seabed by an enterprising Malteser. Pumped out, cleaned up, she was concreted into the dock at Msida and turned into a bar and restaurant. So far so good. But Msida Creek's a bit unfashionable for the local glitterati so business could have been livelier. Until Alex and Maria realised that they were surrounded by thirsty yachties and that if they could get a crowd in regularly, the rest would follow. Now what would do that? Free booze of course. So Wednesday night's Free Wine event was born. Nobody on the pontoons could believe it. Free wine until midnight. Francis Portelli's trade (bad, bad...) in crates of Cisk slumped even further, at least on Wednesdays. Thursdays just no longer existed.

And then? Get a DJ in, let's have some music. Ev'rybody dance! And then? How about a belly dancer? What, not Nige's Fat Prostitute from round the corner? No, thank Cisk, they found a blonde Canadian dancer with seven veils and seventeen piercings, of which you could only see sixteen. Late one Thursday afternoon just after emerging from his bed Ian told me the seventeenth had been spotted some time before dawn that morning.

Beer, it's not just for breakfast

But some people didn't really take to the Black Pearl. If your whole metabolism has been inured to beer for the last thirty years, then cheap Italian plonk, free or not, just doesn't cut it. Our friends Nige and Al are of this persuasion and their main aim is to sample the bars and the beer all the way round the world.

I thought it might save them time and expense if they had a bar on their boat so I suggested this modification for them.

INSTEAD OF PURCHASING A WINDVANE STEERING SYSTEM, NIGE & AL INSTALLED A MORE VITAL PIECE OF EQUIPMENT

In sickness and in health

Did I mention that I broke my collar bone in Malta? Fell down the companionway in a Force 10? Smashed against the rigging climbing up the mast in a raging sea? Well no, I fell off my bike.

I won't go into all sorts of detail about why it really wasn't my own daft fault, but it involves bravado, gear cables rusting through, loss of balance and dignity, very hard concrete and a single life-altering instant, changing me from urban mountain biker to walking wounded. Because after some encouragement ('Get up you pillock, we're going shopping. What's up with you?') and a couple of paracetomols I did finally get on my feet and walk to the hospital.

You can see Sptar San Luca (St Luke's Hospital) from Msida Marina. A huge 1930s blocky building (those stone Lego bricks again) with a tall chimney belching black smoke and oily smuts over all below. Including your nice clean deck. And what do they burn in hospitals? My friend Ian told me.

In A & E's urine-fragrant waiting room we were treated with a cheerful, efficient informality. 'Go in that door and ask for Joey.' Joey, all toothy grin and bottle-bottom glasses and seated at a battered desk in a corridor with peeling cream-painted walls, handed me a slip of paper and sent me off for treatment. The treatment room contained three teenagers in white coats pretending to be doctors, giggling and sprawling across a table. The only other person was a worried-looking woman in an overcoat.

Suddenly we all heard the distinctive moan of a foghorn. The idle chatter stopped. We looked out of the window at the sunshine. Fog? In Malta? The foghorn moaned again. The woman rummaged in her bag and pulled out a mobile phone. The foghorn suddenly stopped as she flipped the phone open and moaned back at it. There was now a distinct air of suppressed hilarity in the room. A teenage boy got up from the table and pressed my shoulder till it hurt, mainly I think to stop him laughing out loud. He told me my collarbone was fractured, strapped me up and sent us off to walk back to the boat. Carefully.

After three or four weeks of enforced idleness, during which I did a lot of drawings for *On the nose*, my bones had knitted together and I was allowed to go for physiotherapy, where I met Laura the Physio, who not only gave me shoulder exercises but took on my perennial back problems too.

Laura didn't mess about. Her approach to the initial appraisal of my physiology was to get the first insults in quickly thus gaining the upper hand. 'Your stance is all wrong! You walk like a pregnant duck! Look at your stomach! I s'pose your chest's alright… yeah, your chest's not bad. Alright (resigned sigh), let's see what we can do.'

So with Laura's thorough and painstaking help, I survived. But others who came to Malta didn't.

Ollie's last pub

Up in Valletta is the pub where Oliver Reed drank his last round on earth before keeling over, on his way to order the next round from that great Barman in the sky. He got through three bottles of Captain Morgan Jamaica Rum, eight bottles of German beer, and a good few doubles of Famous Grouse. He was on a break during the filming of *Gladiator* and despite being 61 had just arm-wrestled five Royal Navy sailors into defeat. Way to go, as they say.

If he'd been buried in Malta and not in Ireland, he might well have gone in this groovy hearse we saw outside the church at the head of Msida Creek.

All in one go? What if it gets dark?

That's enough about Malta, you'll be fed up with it by now. It was Spring, it had stopped raining and it was time to head for the Ionian, our first stop. You can either day sail and coast hop, back to Sicily then along the sole of Italy's foot, or you can go straight from Valletta to the Ionian to clear customs at Kefallinia, Zakynthos or Ithaca, a trip of three days and two nights. Nights? What? Sail overnight? When it's dark? Are you out of your mind?

Some people who have boats in the Med approach night sailing with some trepidation, and some won't do it at all. I think I know why. Stand on the shore at night watching the breakers crash onshore, and you see a faint lonely light crawling along the horizon in the vast lonely infinity of overwhelming blackness, and you think 'Poor brave buggers, out there all on their own in the dark night. Must be terrifying. Rather them than me. Let's go and have another drink.'

Well, it's not quite like that. As dusk falls your eyes become adjusted to the dark. You can fix your position quite accurately by the flashing lights you'll see along the coast, and you'll see that cargo ship bearing down on you a lot sooner than in daylight by watching its lights. And it's rarely ever pitch black. It's best when there's a full moon - we check the moonrise and set times on the GPS. If there's no moon but it's a clear sky full of brilliant stars you can have a magical night.

And there are only a few trips where you'll really need to do overnighters: Menorca to Sardinia, Sardinia to Sicily, Malta to the Ionian, Crete to Cyprus if you're heading that far east. Even Lebanon isn't that far from Cyprus. Depending on how Israel feels about it you could pop into Beirut for a glass of mint tea, and sample the wonderful Lebanese food. Then you could come back via Egypt, and even visit our new chum the Colonel in Libya. Pierre Valti the Swiss sailmaker in Malta goes there for his summer cruises.

So OK, let's give it a go. But wait a sec, what's the wind doing? Is it rough out there? Can we go yet? Better get a forecast…

'A very queer thing is the wind'

How right John Masefield was. So however queer the wind is, let's check out what it's up to. But if you've read *On the nose* you'll know that the Meltemi, the Mistral, the Tramontana, the Khamsin and countless other ancient Mediterranean winds don't actually exist any more, and were replaced by three synthetic winds, the Surlenez (On the nose), the Intrafundamentale (Up the chuff) and the Nofuchinaventi (Buggerall).

These, and the remarkable Ventomatico wind synthesiser that powered and controlled them, were developed by Pan Med Wind Gods, a consortium that took over the wind lease from Aeolus, the original Wind God, who finally couldn't cope with all the different winds with their tedious and enervating idiosyncrasies (tell me if I'm talking too posh for you) and retired to a cottage on the Isle of Wight*.

The system worked well for a few years, and made a decent profit for PMWG and their consortium partners Pan-Mediterranean Turistico Organizacione Marinara Internationale di Marketing Européenne. But the once-satisfied shareholders (mainly investment bankers who found the proverbial trough was no longer big enough for their snouts) were clamouring for more return on their enormous investments (which in the case of Fett Grady Barztidz Inc even exceeded their annual bonuses).

PMWG had originally considered purchasing cheaper, less reliable, imported winds but the original Ventomatico technology couldn't handle them. But PMWG found that their research into celestial particle physics allied to recent developments in chaos theory paved the way to controlling huge volumes of wind energy on a massive scale. So they could import, for example, a typhoon off the coast of Java, split it into manageable chunks, process it and serve up a few dozen pretty realistic Mediterranean winds. With the addition of features such as a sprinkling of red dust for the Harmattan, or a hint of garlic and Côtes de Provence for the Mistral they could fool just about anybody. Though as time went on some

*Just near Ryde it was. Very nice. And it wasn't too dear. You could see the sea out of his bathroom window if you stood on the toilet seat.

of the more sophisticated yachtsmen developed a nose for the 'venti nueve' as they came to be called and became wind connoisseurs.

Anyway, by harnessing internet technology PMWG were soon able to upload data from their new Tiempomatico weather synthesiser to the big weather computers in the USA, thus ensuring 100% accurate GRIB files downloadable by anyone. Finally, by working with Nepseidon Labs, itself a joint enterprise between the Roman and Greek Gods of the Sea, they resolved forever any mismatch between wind and wave activity, ushering in the current totally perfect weather forecasting that we enjoy today in the Mediterranean. And a technology that could be licensed to any other sea area around the globe. The investment bankers were rolling on their backs waving their trotters in the air with glee.

So don't worry about the wind - it's all under control.

But who's in charge?

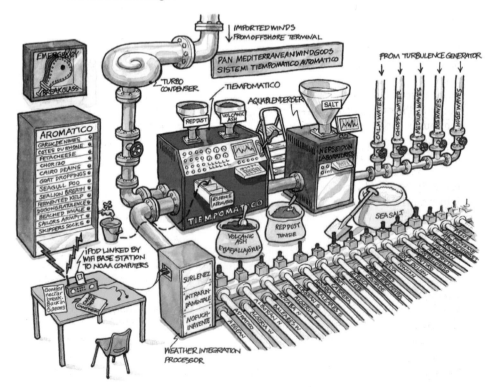

The female skipper

What, a woman in charge of a boat? Whatever next? It may seem a strange thing, but there are lots of women who go on the professional sailing courses, and go on to get jobs in the yachting industry, some as skippers of whacking great mega-yachts.

But it's usually retired couples who go off and live together on a boat, the wife following her husband's mad, irresponsible, uncomfortable and probably dangerous dream because it's the only way she can keep an eye on him. In the pursuit of this dream, the husband has usually spent most of his spare time for years and years messing around in boats, sailing, repairing, even building the dream yacht in the back garden, while his wife has been glad to get him out of the way so she can get on with all that other menial unimportant stuff like having babies, getting the dinner, washing up, gardening or pursuing a high-level career in marketing, politics or brain surgery.

Years of role reinforcement, coupled with the rule which state that there can only be one skipper on a boat, create carte blanche for some husbands to fall into what I call the 'My boat' syndrome, or even the 'Little Admiral' syndrome. You'll spot them. Big, loud, and often the ex-Commodore of the Yacht Club. Their wives respond in various ways depending on the interpersonal dynamics of the couple, ranging from approaches such as 'I'm a doormat, use me' to 'You can let the boat heel like that for the next half hour, but then you have to make it nice and level again so I can do lunch' to 'I'm damned if I'm coming on your feckin' boat again so sling yer hook.' Given this situation, in a lot of yachties' minds the words 'female' and 'skipper' will therefore go together like 'politician' and 'honest', or 'tarantula' and 'cuddly', or… you get my drift.

Both Liz and I used to run businesses so we saw each other as equals and never adopted the 'I'll go out and club the sabre tooth tiger, you cook it' roles. We never joined a Yacht Club either and, coming to sailing quite late, we had no preconceived ideas about living on board. We only knew that it would take another few years of summer holiday charters to get the confidence to sail away in our own boat, so we had to do something.

While we planned all this sell up and sail stuff I was still working full-time, but Liz had the opportunity to go on the 17-week UKSA course on the Isle of Wight, where she gained a Yachtmaster ticket with Commercial endorsement. This saved us a lot of time as I tunnelled my way out of the business world. It also gave her a lot more experience than me, and thus she became... wait for it... wait for it... the Skipper.

So how did I cope with a female Skipper, particularly one I was married to? Well, it was quite simple really; it was excruciatingly bloody difficult.

If neither of you is used to taking orders, you have to find ways of dealing with it. We tried various strategies such as shouting, screaming, verbal abuse, threats, long glum silences and throwing things. A typical marriage you might say. Luckily, before we got to Stage 2: Advanced Strategies (you know, flogging, keel-hauling, dismembering and throwing to the sharks, etc) we found each other's strengths. Liz is good at boat handling in marinas, I'm better at night sailing; Liz is more resilient to seasickness than me, I'm the one who can go up the mast; Liz is good at sail planning, I'm better at sail twitching; the list goes on.

So after five years and a few thousand miles on Yanina, we adopt these roles automatically, and if any flogging occurs it's kept strictly between consenting adults.

The great thing is that this pair of bickering old farts is well looked after by Yanina, our solid, safe and reliable home. And she never argues.

I think I thaw Ithaca

Anyway, I digress. The Ionian. The thing about a sea voyage of more than a day is that when you get into port you really feel you've earned it. You've not just hopped onto a plane and quaffed the duty-free and the micro-waved chicken till touchdown ('Flight attendant, this chicken is rubbery' 'This is Bryanair, sir. I'm afraid we charge extra to laugh at crap old jokes.'). You've navigated your way safely, you've been in control of your own vessel, you've weathered a blow or two, and you've chilled your own white wine in your own fridge and roasted your own chicken in your own oven.

Once we'd reached the headland on the northern tip of Ithaca and turned south for Vathi harbour we got our reward for three long days (and nights) at sea: our sails filled, we hauled in the sheets, and in a steady wind and a flat sea Yanina leaned over and shouldered her way through the water like a rugby forward going for the touchline, in a glorious close reach, as if she wanted one last fling before getting into harbour.

After a whole winter in Malta, your first sight of the Ionian smacks you between the eyes. The islands are so very green and so very beautiful. The Greek speech is a shock to the ear, and the Maltese sing-song lilt to English conversation

is a dusty memory. The old Greek women in black dresses kneeling in prayer in the tiny churches look to Constantinople, not to Rome. You might think it's a subtle difference but a three-day sea voyage makes it quite clear. Stone to leaves. West to East. Catholic to Orthodox.

On a monastery door on a hill top on Ithaca, we saw this sign on the church door. It just seems to sum up all things Greek to me.

Just up from Ithaca is Meganisi ('Big Island'). It is of course tiny. We met this equally tiny woman sweeping the side of the road. I think she'd already done her own yard and her neighbour's and was going to sweep all the way to Spartahori. We swapped a few smiles and words and pointed to the camera. 'Ah. Fotografia.' She struck an instant pose, and we had a great picture. Having just stolen her image, and feeling generous, I offered a euro coin. She looked down and said: 'Ena euro? Ena euro? Another!' Supermodels. You can never pay them enough. Meanwhile down in the village, the Meganisi version of Tesco Online delivery van drivers politely swapped advice on the Greek Highway Code.

Climb out of the village to the hill top, listen to the wind in the pines and the olive trees, look across to the other islands sleeping across the water, and you experience a deep sense of timelessness. These islands will be slumbering in the glittering 'wine-dark sea' for the next few millennia just as they did when Ulysses first slipped his lines from the Customs quay in Vathi.

Stroll back to port, breathing the scent from wild thyme and oregano, musing on the ancient Greeks, the Phoenician sailors, the Venetians, the power of Byzantium, the endless struggle between the Crescent and the Cross. Back into your boat, with a glass of retsina and a few olives to hand, you dig out that book of Greek myths you always meant to start…

… and you hear an English voice on the VHF:

'Komitis Komitis Komitis, this is Kalamari Kalamari Kalamari. Is that you on the left or are you next to the big powerboat? Over.'

'No actually, we're just in front of the boat with the big green thingummy on the back. You coming over for drinkies? Er… over.'

Yes, the flotillas are here. The Ionian is a wonderful place to experience sailing somewhere where you don't need a sprayhood, oilies, or a Mars bar every half hour to keep your core body temperature above freezing. Navigate by the 'point and go' method, then drop the hook in gin-clear water, jump off the back for a swim, and dry off in the sun while you enjoy a cold beer and a Greek salad. The wind is predictable, discreetly allowing you to sleep off your hangover from last night's retsina overload, and easing into a gentle north-westerly by the afternoon, dropping again at sundown. Levkas, Kefallinia, Ithaca and Zakynthos

shield this giant boating lake from the rigours of the open Mediterranean, creating the perfect place for beginners to learn the ropes. Go in September when the Ionian Regatta takes place, and you can race round a small island with up to 200 sailing vessels from windsurfers to ancient wooden gaffers and then, like the rest

of the crews, get thoroughly rat-arsed that same evening. It's perennially organised by a dyed-blond cheerfully-ageing teenager called Robbie, who moors his ancient motor launch at the finish line, Land of Hope and Glory blaring out of two huge speakers.

We want to go back there.

Eventually.

Learning the ropes

So if you *do* want to learn to sail somewhere nice and warm and sunny like the Ionian, go and see Allan Gauci. Years ago he set up what is now Sunvil Sailing, and he and his skippers have taught countless would-be sailors, including us, how to sail and have a lot of fun at the same time.

Allan calls himself a Mediterranean mongrel. Of Maltese, English, Lebanese, Greek and Italian parentage, he grew up in Egypt, and has impressively frightening stories of how, as a child in 1956, he was handed out through a bathroom window to escape the soldiers when the British were turfed out of Egypt by Nasser.

'I love Greece', says Allan. 'They invented democracy here, y'know.' He proves it with a great story, one of many, about when he was in the Greek Merchant Navy. As a new recruit, he found the toilet in his cabin was blocked (you see, it happens on big ships as well as yachts).

He went to the captain to report it, and was told to wait in his cabin and someone would be along shortly to unblock it.

Five minutes later the door opened and a bucket and brush appeared, closely followed by... the captain. Nobody else. Rolling his sleeves up and getting down on his knees, the Greek captain, the Master of this cargo vessel of several thousand tons, rolled his sleeves up and proceeded to use the manual method of unblocking the toilet. Within minutes he was flushed with success. Turning to Allan with a grin, he held out the bucket and brush, and said 'There. It's cleared. Now you know how to do it next time.'

'That's democracy in action' says Allan.

His sailing courses operate on the same democratic principles of course...

30

The moor the merrier

In Malta we realised we'd been ploughing up sea beds from Scotland to Italy, dragging our boat (our home) around the anchorage behind our somewhat inadequate 25lb CQR* anchor. Imagine coming home after a trip to ASDA to find your bungalow isn't where you left it, but wedged up against the roundabout at the bottom of the road.

Get a heavier CQR then? Well yes, but a CQR's a plough anchor. And what do ploughs do? Plough a furrow. OK for planting your spuds but not to hold your boat in place. You need something that digs in straightaway and just holds. If the wind changes and it pulls out, you want it to dig in again straightaway and hold just as firmly. Simple as that. Any other anchors then? Yes, there's the Danforth, Bruce, Delta, Bügel, Spade, Fortress, Manson, Rocna and the engagingly-named Bulwagga. The best performing

anchors had two features: a roll bar to make the anchor turn into the seabed in the first place, and a *concave* blade, like a sharp-pointed spoon, to dig in straightaway.

At the time the only anchor that had both these was the Rocna, available from New Zealand. But we were in Malta. This would be expensive, but then so is insurance and you buy that every year. And what's the best insurance for a boat? A bloody good anchor that you can trust. We bought it, and we haven't dragged anchor since. Honest.

In small Greek harbours there's no room to lie alongside, so you drop your bow anchor, reverse in at right angles and slot in between the other boats like sardines in a tin. Then you can get out the G & Ts and Pringles and pose in your aft cockpit, impressing the locals and the tourists alike. Unlike modern fin keel boats, Yanina can't reverse in a straight line so we always go in forward, dropping our smaller anchor, our kedge, from the stern. With our bows to the wall we can't pose in the cockpit but then we have more privacy, and it's much harder for a thief to clamber on board. Of course it's harder for us too especially when we return, tired as newts, at four in the morning. So…

*An acronym for 'Comes (out) Quite Rapidly

31

… we have a plank on board. Now I can hear you cruisers say: 'Yeah, we've got a plank on board. His name's Brian.' But you know that's not what I mean. We use the plank to get ashore. If we had a bigger posher boat we'd have a 'passerelle' which is a bigger and posher plank made out of aluminium. They both do the same job but one can cost the price of an inflatable dinghy, a much better investment for your euros, while the other can be made from a sawn-off length of scaffolding plank, an offcut of stainless steel tube* (which in our case I found in a skip), a bit of 6mm line and some bungee, sometimes known as shock cord. A simple but clever idea from Nige on Strummer.

And the great thing is that you can ease your boat away from the quay, thus saving more bangs on the nose when some ignorant sod zooms past in a power boat. You can haul it up at night when you go to bed, so any thief will have to leap across and hang on to the anchor before he can get a foot on board. In the 'down' position, the plank hovers above the quay, or the wooden pontoon if you're in a marina. Less chance of cockroaches or rats coming aboard, and you can hear the thump when somebody steps on your plank.

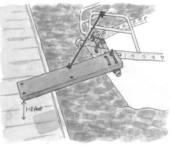

Unfortunately it's a great toy for small boys to jump up and down on, but they soon get tired of it. And if they don't, just tie a nice big sailbag to your spare halyard and enjoy a game of marina skittles…

*I was told recently by a stainless steel fabricator that there is no such thing as an offcut, but that stainless steel tube comes in long lengths or short lengths, and they're all bloody expensive.

Advanced anchoring techniques

In *On the nose* I described the French anchoring technique of dropping an anchor directly over yours, then leaping ashore for one of those disgusting aniseed-flavoured drinks that remind them of the good old days when you could go blind drinking absinthe. Well, they've developed another method that gets the anchor to actually bite into the seabed and not just lie about on it in an existential torpor as if waiting for the next glassful of oblivion. So this is hugely advanced stuff for the French.

A French boat charged round the headland into our peaceful anchorage at full whack. The anchor was dropped and out rattled a generous amount of chain. With a flick of ze wrist, ze skipper he jam on ze brake on ze windlass*, ze chain it go tight as ze Lady Gaga's bra strap, ze anchor she dig in. Ze yacht she do a petit pirouette and then she make ze stop, rocking madly fore-and-aft. Voilà. It was only then that they broke out the Ricard and the 'Crunchy Frog'-flavoured crisps.

But why stop there? There's a German yacht going around the Med with its main anchor on the stern. The wind blows them into an anchorage, they steer over a nice bit of sand, drop the hook off the back and just stop, facing *downwind*. None of that tedious turning head to wind, engine on, reversing and paying out the correct amount of chain, and gunning the engine to set the anchor.

Now ever since the first innovative coracle-owner tied a big lump of rock onto a long rope and chucked it overboard to halt his progress downwind, the anchor has always been on the pointy end. In the Irish Sea or the Baltic you want your cockpit well protected from

*Windlass does not refer to a flatulent girl from Yorkshire, but is the mechanism which winds the chain and anchor back onto your boat and gives you a bad back in the process.

wind, rain and spray, and you're quite happy that your boat faces into the wind. But in the summer heat of the Med yachties go to great lengths to achieve a flow of air through into the saloon, compromising the safety of their hatches at sea by making them open forward, tying wind scoops above them, and still needing

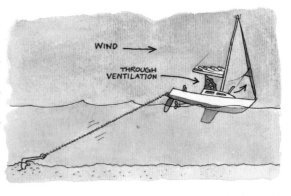

electric fans below. This German skipper realised that his aft cockpit and sprayhood made a huge efficient wind scoop as long as his boat faced downwind. He had asked the question 'Why' to a long-accepted methodology and found a benefit in putting his big hook on the back of the boat.

But does this work in the winter? Cold driving rain lashing into the cockpit? Keep all your washboards in? Can't be right. What does he do? Lock the boat in a marina and fly off to Florida or the ski resorts, that'd be the best thing. Sod all this sailing in the cold and wet.

Don't chuck it in a bucket

So, you have your super modern seabed-biting anchor, your equally tenacious kedge anchor, your plank and your Advanced Anchorers badge. But whatever anchor you have, it won't work if it's not on the seabed. Where else is it going to be, you ask? Another cruising couple we met in Turkey, Paul and Kit, told us of

their experience of anchoring in a delightful little bay for five weeks, dinghying ashore for trips inland, and leaving the boat for quite long periods.

They were about to go ashore again when the weather changed and the Meltemi kicked in. They dragged anchor straightaway, the boat moving rapidly towards some ruggedly picturesque-looking rocks. Nothing for it but to get the engine on, weigh anchor and re-set it. The anchor came up easily but seemed quite heavy. Strange... It cleared the water, and hooked neatly on it was an ancient bucket full of mud. That's what had held ten tons of boat in place for five weeks.

But look on the bright side. At least they now had a spare bucket.

The art of communication

The VHF radio - what would we do without it? Back to Morse code and semaphore I guess. Some might think VHF is just a sort of phone on the boat that lets you call your friends for free. So it is, but it's also the basic means of communication between ships, boats, Coast Guard, and emergency services. Not many people know that van Gogh was one of the first users of early VHF radio.

VHF is what's called 'open channel', which means the rest of the marina, or anchorage, or anyone else with a VHF set, like for example, the Coast Guard, the Customs, the marina office, can hear every word you say. We've heard confidential conversations about an epidemic of nits, about the idiosyncrasies of the marina manager, and about the avoidance of the dreaded Spanish 'boat tax'.

There are channels with different frequencies for commercial or other use but there's an agreed 'hailing channel' in every marina, say 67 or 68. Once you've made contact on that you switch to a different channel for a chat, leaving the hailing channel clear. But as soon as you say 'Go to 72?' to your chum so you can have a 'private' conversation, you should know that scores of other nosey yachties will surreptitiously 'go to 72' too. After all it's only human nature - everyone likes to earwig.

The emergency channel is 16, and you only use that to call another boat, and then leave it clear by switching to a different channel for your conversation. During the day most people are pretty good at doing this, but listening on 16 on your overnight passage you'll hear the bored crew of cargo ships and tankers on night watch play music (not allowed), belch (definitely not allowed), swear and insult each other on a regular basis (definitely, definitely out of the question).
Happens every night.

Meteora on the rocks

Some people only think of Greece as the islands. But the mainland offers so much. You want ancient ruins? You've come to the right place. We don't go in for that much. Reconstituting a civilisation together in your mind from a pile of stones in the hot sun surrounded by Japanese tourists is not easy. But some places can't be missed, and Meteora is one of them.

It's not an ancient ruin, but a whole rocky landscape of living working monasteries, built in the fourteenth century. If there's one thing the Greeks do well it's monasteries; they've got thousands of them, but the ones at Meteora are special. They perch precariously on the tops of a series of remarkable natural sandstone towers, looking like something out of Tolkien.

We left our boat at Nidri, on Levkas, and rented a car with some friends. It's a day's drive from Nidri to Kalambaka, where you can find places to stay near the monasteries. Ignoring the expensive hotels we drove round and asked at some places where, to paraphrase Groucho, I wouldn't want to stay if they were willing to have me as a guest. Then in a square on the edge of town, we wearily stopped in front of the Koka Roka Pension. A shambling figure shuffled towards us from the gloom, stopped and surveyed us (oh dear, it's a Greek Lurch). Before I could impress this simple native with my extensive Greek vocabulary and say 'Buenas tardes, Stavros, haben sie ena domatio parakalo?' we heard 'G'day mates! Need some rooms? Doin' a barbie later, d'ya like goat?'

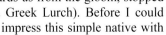

This was delivered in perfect Strine. We had just met Arthur, our host for the next two days, who had misspent his youth in Sydney, then returned to his family in later years, as the Greeks do. Αφανασιυσ was his real name, after the local saintly person but nobody bothered with that, not even his mum. So after a goat-munching session and a few tinnies with Arthur that evening, we spent the next two days gawping and gasping at the monasteries, each one perched on top of its vertiginous rock tower, the best protection you could get from marauding infidels (those Turks again I'm afraid).

So how did they all get up there? Often the way up for a new monk was to be hauled up in a net. The winding mechanisms are still in place in some of them. One novice monk (clearly a potential Health & Safety officer) apparently asked when the rope was replaced.

'When it breaks.'

Leaving was another matter. In this ossuary, shelf upon shelf of skulls had been collected over the centuries (I guess the rest of the bones had been sold to the Italians to make relics). So there was only one way out of the monastery. At least it would save wear on the rope.

We managed to escape back to Nidri with our skulls still attached, and with only a minor detour taken during a free and frank but friendly discussion with our friends Alan and Doreen about the role (and indeed financing) of the Royal Family in Britain today. Just as I was saying how Prince Charles was the same age as me (it's bizarre but true) and why should *he* get all the breaks and not me, it's really so unfair after I've worked hard all my life and he just wanders round with one hand stuffed in his jacket pocket talking about carbuncles and organic biscuits - just then our attention was diverted, and high in the mountains, we crossed a river we shouldn't have, spent five hours in first gear along a winding dirt track, forded several streams and reached the road by bouncing through a tunnel still under construction.

'Where've you been?' said Homer of Homer Rentacar back in Nidri. 'Driving along Igoumenitsas beach?' as he surveyed the dust on his Korean fartbox. As we didn't know where Igoumenitsas was we couldn't answer so we quietly walked back to our boats. Enough of trudging through the dust. Time to go sailing.

Time to go sailing

That's easy to say isn't it? Time to go sailing. Time to... But is it time? Should we or shouldn't we? And where to? What's the forecast? Is the boat ready? Should I do an oil change? Will we run out of tonic and lemons? Can I be arsed anyway?

When cruising in the Med, the stress is just constant: you face a difficult dynamic decision every day. Shall we stay here and just laze around, shall we go to the next bay and just laze around there, or shall we miss that one and go to the one that looks much nicer for lazing around but is more than a day's sail away? Some people have been cruising the Med for years facing these enormous challenges day in day out; they must be nervous wrecks by now.

And so it was around the Peloponnese, where we were heading next. There are so many lovely little harbours and anchorages. Can you see them all? Do you have to? Or do you get a wiggle on and think 'I've got to be in Barbados by next Christmas, can't hang around here faffin' about.'

This is what happens when you choose to travel round the world at six miles an hour. There's so much to see and so little time, particularly when you realise that most cruisers are crumblies who'll never see 50 again, let alone 60, and even when they actually get somewhere they can't remember why they wanted to in the first place. This is commonly known as Cruizheimer's Disease. Now what was I saying? Oh yes... Time to... Time to go...

But before we slip our lines let's have another quick look at our fellow anchorage dwellers and marina neighbours. Most of us yachties are really quite normal apart from the fact that we've chosen this floating way of life. But as in any community there are those for whom normality is a bit of a challenge.

Midnight Cruiser

We all like to stay up chatting into the small hours, but sound carries amazingly across the water. When the Midnight Cruiser wants a good old chinwag he takes advantage of this so that he can broadcast his views on life to those around him. But a polite request to desist from his nocturnal ramblings usually does the trick.

The Meerkat

He was pointed out to me by Rob and Brenda, on Paprika. Often a singlehander, usually a little bit dotty, he will pop up in an instant, tense, alert, eyes darting to and fro, nostrils quivering, on the lookout for transgressions, misbehaviour or just anything really.

He knows exactly who arrived when and who's about to leave and where they're heading, even before they do. But he's basically harmless, just like our next Cruising Character...

The Marina Prat

In every marina where there are enough liveaboards there's usually one of these. They do come in different types so you'll have to spot yours for yourself. My benign nature, generosity of spirit and sympathetic feelings for my fellow man, but mainly the libel laws, prevent me from saying where we spotted this example. Interesting features though. Ex-Army Officer; thoroughly rude to everyone. And he's always willing to give advice. He'll leap aboard any new arrival's boat without a moment's hesitation and tell them exactly what's wrong with it.

Note the accessories, for this is a Marina Prat with a bike. Miniature fenders so that cars that stray too close will simply bounce off him, mudguards lovingly carved from re-cycled plastic water bottles, and the symbolic purple helmet. We do need people like this. Just to remind us.

But let's drag ourselves away from the marina and its characters. There are places to see, time is passing and there's bound to be another Prat in the next marina.

Three fingers to you

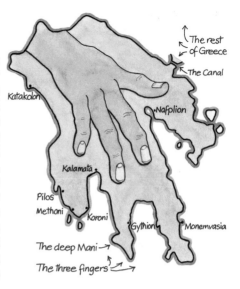

You can head east from the Ionian through the Corinth Canal, but you pay a hefty fee for the privilege. And that sizeable chunk of Greece that the canal lops off quite neatly is the Peloponnese. On the chart this looks like a strangely-proportioned hand with three stumpy fingers and a thumb, and you can't help wondering what's on the end of those fingers. It's all very intriguing. There were three reasons to go for it: some friends had advised us not to miss the Peloponnese; the wind would be an *Intrafundamentale* (from behind) for a lot of the way; there was no canal fee to pay. We headed south.

Our first stop on the Peloponnese was at Katakolon. What a weird place that was. A massive quay, an unfinished concrete marina, just a set of decaying wooden fingers with no power, and one water tap in a hole in the ground. A sleepy one-street town with shops full of tourist tat, empty bars and restaurants, and a puzzlingly enormous empty car park.

But when the cruise liner docked at mid-day, the place lurched into action like some kind of giant Hellenic music box. Shops thronged, bars heaved, restaurants burst into rings of Greek dancing to the perennial strains of Zorba the Greek, and the car park was stuffed with scores of shiny air-conditioned coaches ready to cart the cruise line punters off to Olympia just down the road. And then at about three o'clock, Katakolon just shut down and went back to sleep.

We bought an English paper to catch up on world politics and current affairs. The headlines read 'Heather and Macca porn shock' and inside I read that Harrods' latest accessory for your post-modern minimalist bathroom was black toilet paper at £4.95 for six rolls. Very reasonable, and a practical colour too. Perhaps they'd fly some out to the boat?

The next day, our sails goose-winged out, we were pushed along by the *Intrafundamentale* to Pilos, another unfinished concrete marina but a pretty harbour and village in a bay so well-sheltered that they held the Battle of Navarino here in 1827. Much more civilised than tossing around in the open sea.

The coast around here was almost a miniature version of that around Almeria in Andalucia. Limestone hills behind a sloping plain. Greenhouses here and there, but small in scale, in harmony with the landscape. No vast dusty sea of plastic. No cheap Moroccan labour of course. As if to confirm that we weren't in Andalucia we got our first glimpse of an Aegean blue-domed church.

Oh, for the wings, for the wings of a goose

Down the outside of the Peloponnesian hand to the little finger we whizzed, at a comfortable six knots, dead downwind with the chuckling waves running along beside us, full genoa on one side and full mainsail on the other, for that is what goose-winging is. Our windyometer told us that we had apparently 25 knots of wind on our backs, pleasantly cooling in the hot sun. If we'd stopped suddenly, say, by hitting a reef, we'd have felt the 31 knots that it was truly blowing. And full mainsail and full genoa would no longer be a good idea. So Apparent Wind can be very different from True Wind. If we'd really hit a reef we'd of course be thoroughly pissed off and seriously considering buying a motorhome.

This is why goose-winging dead downwind is such a pleasant but dangerous activity. If you lose concentration and go off course, and you've forgotten your preventer*, the wind will snatch your boom, whip it over uncontrollably and knock you out of the cockpit, those chuckling waves will get even more friendly and try to splash their way into the cockpit, and your genoa will be trying to rip itself to shreds like a goose's wing just after a close encounter with a jumbo jet. So steer very carefully or you can get thoroughly goosed.

*A line that pulls your boom forward and prevents a gybe. A gybe? Oh, google it yourself.

Past Methoni with its ruined Turkish fortress and its Venetian castle that looked like a giant sandcastle, we didn't stop till we'd rounded the foothills of the headland of the little finger of the Peloponnese and got to Koroni, a sleepy little town with a small headland that you can just tuck yourself behind out of the wind. Damn. Someone had got the best spot before us. Rather grumpily we dropped the hook on the edge of the bay. I glanced across at the other boat. Somehow it looked familiar. I looked again. Good grief. Another Warrior 35, same colour, same sail cover, same dinghy, same radar, same radar reflector. It was like looking in a giant mirror. Who would we find on board? Us?

Fortunately it wasn't us or our döppelgangers. We had met Ian and Heather. Great! We could sail up the coast together and I could ask Ian if he too had a rusty home-made wrench with a small square bit on the end and what on earth did he use it for (he didn't), or whether he had got within 3 feet of their stern gland without hacking out half the cockpit floor (he hadn't). As a bonus we got Heather's many smallholding stories, including the one when she had dashed out at night in nothing but her wellies to help her cow to calf.

Heather's stories and the look of this coast made us nostalgic for North Wales, particularly the view from above Pwllheli or from Rhiw mountain over Snowdonia and the Cardigan Bay. Approaching Petalidhion there was even a mountain just like Rhiw with an aerial mast. It was cloudy, cold, with thunder and lightning. Just like Wales then.

We crossed over to Kalamata marina, entering just as a squall began to pass over us. Now came one of those 'If only we…' or 'We should have known that…' or 'Why the feck didn't we…' moments. A spotty youth waved us into a particularly awkward berth, Liz gunned the engine as you have to in Yanina, and the cross-wind took our brand new Rocna anchor onto another boat's stanchion just before we tied up. They're tough those Rocna's. Tougher than stanchions anyway.

Too much democracy

Which is how I got to talk to the stainless steel man (working out how much we'd have to pay) and heard about the unfinished marinas. He looked German, cropped hair and an old Mercedes in perfect nick, but he spoke rapid Greek to the marina manager on his mobile. Back in the marina office, he said he *was* Greek but born and raised in Germany, and was more comfortable with the German ethic than the Greek.

'There's too much democracy in Greece, everybody does just what they please, nobody cares.' 'But you didn't have too much democracy in the 70s under the colonels.' 'My father said it was good, you went to an office and the man stood up, asked what you needed and did what was necessary. Now it's: I have a headache, come back later, I don't know. But I do like *some* freedom.'

He told me the marina was built with EU money 'like all the marinas round here'. But it was all for a fast buck. Get a few million in, do a cheap job on the concrete, don't finish the marina, don't even think about running it, take the money and run. A big charter company now owned 40% of the marina and had plans to improve it. But the rest of the shareholders owned small amounts, say 7% for the manager, 4% for his brother, 3% for his cousin. They couldn't agree so nothing would happen.

'When you listen to discussions on Greek TV, they don't start from alpha and end with omega, like the Germans; they start with beta, go to epsilon, back to gamma, it's crazy crazy crazy.' This is why he worked on his own.

46

In Kalamata, we rented a little family car from Hellen Rent-a-car, a little family firm ('Hello meester, pliss, slow slow slow and no drinkie'), and took the mountain road to Mistra. Straggly pines, rocks and boulders were strewn across the hillsides as if scattered by some giant hand. A narrow gorge led to Mistra, an entire wooded hillside of Byzantine churches and monasteries tumbling over one another, some half-ruined, surrounded by olives and cypresses and overlooking what once was Sparta.

Trudging up a rocky path we saw flying metallic green beetles as big as your big toe, the sound of their wings like miniature air-cooled flat fours. Crickets whirred away, tiny mechanical monsters. Ants dragged the remains of a cricket like a wrecked car shell, up the side of (to the ants) a 20-foot high stone on the path.

We humans have it easy really.

Manic Mani

You can do pleasant day sails around this indented Peloponnesian middle finger, stopping in quiet anchorages surrounded by stark hills, with the Taigetos mountains as an ever present backdrop. This is the Deep Mani. Tiny villages in small perfectly formed bays are made up of solidly-built four-square stone houses, each with an intriguing tall solidly-built four-square stone tower. Who built them? Why?

In the spirit of generous neighbourliness, a local Maniot villager would build a tower on his house so that he could look down on his irritating neighbour and take a pot shot at them from a safe height without any fear of reprisal. Whereupon his neighbour, rather fed up with this unwanted attention, would build a taller tower and try to shoot the living daylights out of the original perpetrator. Whereupon… and so on and so on until they ran out of stones or sand-and-cement (not a good choice of builders' merchants in Mani) and declared a truce, going back to settling scores by a bout of power dominoes or maybe a spot of arm wrestling.

By then a third neighbour would have nicked some sand-and-cement off the back of a wagon, and built his own tower to shoot both of his noisy squabbling neighbours who were making far too much noise at their dominoes. And so it went on, breaking only to get the harvest in and bury the dead. Life must go on after all.

The butcher with red nails

Up between the second and index fingers was Gythion and its harbour. Houses, some derelict, tumbled down the hillside, cypresses and scrub above them, the Taigetos mountains across the bay. We were in need of minced beef for Liz to make her legendary Spag Blog, so we found the local butcher's shop.

A slender slip of a girl with bright red nails, red lips, bare navel and embroidered slippers languished in the back of the shop, no doubt waiting for her big beefy dad/hubby/ sugar daddy with butcher's fingers like thick sausages to return to hack big lumps of meat to pieces and hurl them at the customers.

But no, our prejudices were confounded. She *was* the butcher. At our request she expertly carved up some quality beef, fed it into the grinder and wrapped the resulting mince in the best Peloponnesian greaseproof paper, handing it over with a smile that had me lusting after her giblets for days afterwards.

Nothing classier than Monemvasia

Round the corner again to Monemvasia. Out on a short limb attached to the mainland, it's a tiny but perfectly formed and preserved medieval walled town with a ruined fortress on the hill above it. A sense of place and history so powerful you could almost smell it. Or maybe that was the goats.

But when you get in there and sample the bars and tourist shops, the place has that overwhelmingly tasteful and cloying sweetness that the Greeks specialise in - the visual equivalent of those baklava pastries with 500 giga-calories in every bite.

Better to step back and see the whole. The ruined hilltop fortress is something else. A zigzag climb through the town and then along a path with a spooky overhead network of spiders' webs stretched from shrub to shrub - not for the arachnophobic, but once breached, yielding the view of the islands you were hoping for. That timelessness again.

Is it me or did I hear the wind getting up?

Katabatic winds

The *Greek Waters Pilot* warned of sudden and unexpected katabatic (what?) winds here at Monemvasia. During the day, in gentle and light airs, you can park your boat in the rudimentary and decrepit harbour, using your kedge anchor to hold you off the pontoons. You sort of wonder why the local fishing boats are all tied up alongside with about twenty old tyres along their beams, but what the feck? It's free! Another cheap overnight stay. Let's have a beer and look up what 'katabatic' means in the Pilot. Let's see... Kalamari ('Here's that sick squid I owe you')... Kalamata, famous for its enormous olives... Kalimera, no that's 'good morning'... Katabatic.

'A katabatic wind is formed when air above high mountains cools by radiation, particularly as the land cools at night. As its density increases, it flows downhill, reaching speeds from 10 knots to hurricane speed.' Right then. But that's only in places like the Arctic. Isn't it?

Sure it is. You just snuggle up in bed and don't worry about it. Then when you half-wake wondering whether you should have put some extra bow fenders on, or made sure your kedge anchor was really really holding, that's when 35 knots of wind instantly coalesces into being, scooting down the mountainside and straight up your chuff, and you find your bow thumping the sharp edge of the quay over and over like a demented but short-sighted ram head-butting a gate. Until you stumble out of bed, fire up the engine and slam it in reverse, thus holding your pride and joy away from further bangs on the nose.

And in 20 minutes it's vanished. The various lumps of cold air and warm air elbowing each other above you have reached uneasy equilibrium again, leaving half a dozen skippers in various states of undress, still with a hand on the throttle lever, looking round in puzzlement. Bang indeed.

Nafplion: smart but smelly

If you head back up the interstice (never sure how to pronounce that) of the index finger and thumb of the Peloponnese (the thumb is the Argolis peninsula) you'll get to a lovely little town called Nafplion, Nafplio, Navplion or Nauplion. In the *Greek Waters Pilot*, Rod Heikell calls it the most civilised town in the Peloponnese and I agree. For a brief moment in history it was the capital of Greece, when Greece was little more than the Peloponnese. Everybody else had the other bits. It's got a charming old quarter, a great beach when the wind's in the right direction, a harbour (free mooring but very, very smelly), and the Palamidi fortress on the top of a handy hill with 999 steps to reach it.

I read that it took the Venetians only four years to build, and was taken in its first siege. It was the shortest siege on record, the Venetians capitulating in less than a week if my memory serves me well. There must be more to that story if it's true. The Italians don't surrender without a good reason.

We busked in Nafplion for the second time in our y a c h t i f i c a t o r y transnavicularisation of the Mediterranean (tell me if I'm still talking too posh for you), and made a huge sum of money, enough to spend on a new set of guitar strings and a pizza.

Not as good as Menorca in the last book but buskers can't be choosers. The best acclaim we got was a 20-something-year-old American tourist (lots of them there) giggling and saying to us in passing: 'You guys are terrific.' I wanted to check the irony level of her comment. She knew we were older than her mom and dad and gee it *was* kind of cute seeing these old Brit farts play for pennies in the street.

Oh well. Today Nafplion, tomorrow the Albert Hall, that's what I think.

Sliding up the Euripus Channel

To get up to the northern Greek mainland we found that Greece's second largest island, Evvoia (a.k.a. Evvia, Evia, Euboea, Euboia or even Negropont if you're from Venice and have a very long memory) was in the way. To avoid the open Aegean and heading straight up into the Meltemi we opted for the Euripus Channel between Evvoia and the mainland. Exit at the top end and then you've half a chance because you'll be heading north-east, and the Meltemi feeds in from the north-west up there. Result: a nice beam reach, a very rare treat in these parts.

It's a kind of river trip, interesting rather than exciting, with quiet unfrequented anchorages giving way to an almost industrial section before you reach the Khalkis Sliding Bridge. Yes, sliding. Clever eh? The bridge would open at 11.30 pm. By eleven we were all set. We waited. And waited. In a kind of watery Musical Chairs, boats started a slow circling of the anchorage, but staying close to the bridge. Half past eleven! Excitement. Tension. Adrenaline. Any second now. Just get in ahead of that ketch, not too close. Damn, go round again. Here we go! Do we? Yes?

No, we don't. The bridge stayed resolutely closed. The traffic resolutely rolled on. Adrenaline drained away into the darkness. At three o'clock I was looking for matches to prop up my eyelids (didn't fancy the cocktail sticks). Suddenly lights flashed, cars braked, engines revved, boats thrashed around. The bridge slid open. Yes! Go for it! No-one wanted to be last. As we passed the bar-restaurant built onto the bridge we only glimpsed lights, figures, faces. It was all over in a few seconds but they were clearly going to party on.

We were through, and suddenly in pitch black, looking for an anchorage chosen

from our out-of-date Pilot book. Using GPS to find our spot just outside a tiny unlit harbour for local boats, I reached for the Steamer Scarer, our 5 billion candle power torch to check how close we were. Click. Nothing. Flat battery. Bugger. We dropped the anchor anyway, dug it in, put the GPS anchor drag alarm on and fell into bed. Daylight found us within 40 metres of a new harbour breakwater that wasn't on our chart or in our Pilot. Thankfully it had been a calm night. A lot of yachties defend their use of out-of-date charts and Pilot books by saying 'Rocks don't move.' Well, they do if a Greek builder's put them there.

Aristotle's tidal downfall

So what was all that about then? Why did we have to stay awake drinking all that coffee for four hours waiting for the bridge to slide open?

Well, the tide flows back and forth four times a day. Just like the Solent then? But it can reach speeds of up to seven knots (and this is in the non-tidal Med). So you have to go past the bridge at slack water. OK, we can all do that, but it's only slack for eight minutes, so to get a couple of dozen boats through means you can't faff about. And don't forget all those impatient Greek drivers leaning on their car horns.

But the plot thickens. On the three days around the first and last quarters

of the moon, the tide can change direction up to 14 times a day or, perversely, do nothing at all. The problem kept Aristotle awake too. It's said that in later years when he retired to Evvoia when the bottom fell out of the philosophy market ('I think therefore I am unemployed'), he was so incensed that he couldn't fathom out why the phenomenon occurred that he jumped into the straits and drowned. Others say he died of a stomach complaint, so my theory is that he swallowed something unmentionable before they fished him out. They'd have to wait up to six hours anyway to let the tide bring him back to the bridge.

But I think the first thing he'd have needed after a stomach pump would be a laundrette.

Or failing that maybe he could benefit from the tips on the next page.

54

Laundry tips

Tip Number 1

Ask yourself: *Do I actually need to wash anything?* Aristotle, you don't need to answer this one. Or to put it another way: *Do I smell yet?* Now I'm not saying (am I? of course I'm not) that yachties are a bunch of filthy, smelly ragged sea-gypsies that you wouldn't want to go downwind of with a peg on your nose, but in hot climates like the Med, living outdoors only wearing T-shirt and shorts, with no thick pullover to hold in the perspiratory effluvia and consequent bacterial activity, (I think I *am* talking too posh for you) a yachtie can sweat in the same T-shirt for a few days and his armpits will still be charmpits (relatively speaking). It's just as well because washing uses up precious water on board. We have a friend who swears that after a couple of weeks in the same T-shirt it just doesn't smell any more, it reaches a sort of olfactory

equilibrium. I can't confirm that because we always made sure we were upwind of him and he's never sailed with us since.

And yachties are not the only ones. Long distance walkers extend the pre-wash period of their underpants, by turning them back-to-front after the first week (or month if you are an advanced or very long distance walker), inside-out after the second week, and front-to-back again but inside-out after the third week. After that they'll probably walk alongside you anyway so you should really throw

them away. As for socks, you just throw them at the mainsail, and if they stick in place you wash them. If they fall off you can put them back on again. But then Mediterranean yachties don't wear socks anyway. It's too hot and it would be a sartorial crime to wear them under your sandals.

Tip Two: When you were at school, when someone asked you what was black, wrinkled and floats in the sea, you were supposed to say Binbag the Sailor. Instead, rescue it from the sea and follow our friend Lisa's tip. Fill it with dirty washing and pour enough soapy water in to soak the washing. Seal the bag, roll it around on deck a bit, then leave it for a day or two. The sun will heat the water, the movement of the boat will gently agitate it, and you can then pull all your stuff out into one of those big floppy plastic buckets to rinse it.

Tip Three: Now that you've washed and rinsed, don't you need a spin drier? Take a drive off your prop shaft to power up a spin drier somewhere in the cockpit? Somebody will do it, now that I've mentioned it. No need. Just follow Lin and Larry Pardey's tip as told to us by Alison on Strummer. Throw your soggy T-shirt around one of the shrouds, grab both ends and twist. If you can think of a way to hold a mop as well you can clean the deck at the same time.

Tip Four: From our Antipodean chum Penny, who's been hanging washing out on board for years. It begins with a bit of obscure nautical history. Everyone knows that the Beaufort Wind Scale, which allocates a number to each level of wind strength and sea state, was originated by Admiral Sir Francis Beaufort, born in Ireland of Huguenot ancestry.

Yes? Well, no actually. He nicked the idea from Fanny Beaufort, his long-suffering spouse. Living on a windy headland with splendid views of the white-capped waves out to sea, she realised that you need a second pair of pegs on the sides of your washing to stop it flipping over the line, and it was a simple step to realise that the stronger the wind, the more pegs she would need if she wasn't to lose her husband's long johns into the sea again. Four pegs: Force 4, moderate breeze. Ten pegs, Force 10, whole gale... simple.

After many years of politely, modestly, but persistently putting this simple but brilliant idea to the top brass at the Admiralty (who hated her husband because he was a bit of a smartarse compared to them, and who ignored her because they thought she was a mere woman and knew nothing about anything) she finally gave in, and said to her husband, 'I give in. I. Give. In. *You* go. *You* damn well go and convince that bunch of stupid ignorant pillocks at the soddin' friggin' Admiralty. You'll stand more chance 'cos you're one of the feckers yourself, you pompous Huguenot arse.'

And so he did. And Fanny insisted that her husband got his just recognition when the scale was named. And thus the Huguenot Arse Wind Scale was born, which the Admiralty were forced to rename as Beaufort when the French tried to claim that *L'Echelle des Vents du Cul d'Huguenot* was their invention.

Synchronisin' on the dock of the bay

Out of the channel at the top of Evvoia to Koukounaries Bay on Skiathos, a beautiful broad bay with a jetty and a tiny harbour in the corner, with clear blue water just inviting you to jump in, white sand equally inviting for the anchor to bite into. An idyllic anchorage. With extras.

Like jet skis. Water skiers. Para gliders. Giant inflatable bananas being towed past by powerful speedboats. I wanted to swim and snorkel to check how well our anchor had dug in but had visions of being chopped in half before I could get there.

So we opened a couple of beers instead. Then the entertainment began. From around the headland a tripper boat cheerfully chugged its way to the jetty, its speakers equally cheerfully blasting out holiday pop. Five red-shirted figures jumped onto the jetty as two more boats rounded the headland and approached, crammed with dancing, screaming, laughing, cheering holidaymakers. The jetty became alive as five grinning red shirts began their synchronised dance routine, bodies whirling, arms waving, legs kicking. On the boats bodies whirled, arms waved, legs kicked. Everyone was having a thumping good time. They all trooped ashore and gradually disappeared up the path to the village, the sound of laughter echoing round the bay. Silence again.

We sipped our beer, feeing very old. When we were twenty did we need a bunch of cheerleaders to tell us we could have a good time? But that was in the 60s. Hang on though, we did have Butlins Redcoats…

Thank goodness for Alexander Papadiamantis, writer and poet, one of Greece's favourites, who grew up in Skiathos. He's got a statue in the harbour. Here's his most famous quotation: 'The eternal human adventure. Is there ever an end to the pains and woes of humankind?'

Too right, Alex. You go and tell those day trippers. And sort the jet skis out while you're at it.

58

On the other hand

A lumpy beam reach took us from Skiathos to Porto Koufo on the middle finger of Greece's other giant hand, the Halkidiki peninsula. I'd always been curious about this since seeing it in a school atlas.

So why did we miss out the first finger? Or, come to that, Thessaloniki, Greece's second largest city. Well, time really. We knew where we had to be for winter and we couldn't see everything along the way. In the first finger's case, I don't think we missed much. It's a collection of beaches, each with a massive sound system, full of Greek holidaymakers. Thessaloniki? We'd been told that it was a big noisy polluted city, which I'm sure it is. Had we read the Rough Planet, we might have called in. There's a lot to see. Alexander the Great was born here and surprisingly so was Atatürk. Mount Olympus is close by, and if you chuck a stone you'll probably hit a major archaeological site. And Thessaloniki is said to be Greece's coolest city, centre of the arts, music and poetry, not to mention its annual Film Festival. Oh well, we'll catch it next time around.

Anyway Porto Koufo was a delight. Go there and anchor. It's the most perfectly sheltered anchorage you could wish for, shaped on the chart like a wrinkled old sock, good holding in sand, and buggerall there but for a few bars and tavernas. Very quiet, very relaxed, and I'll remember it because we met the hairiest man I have ever come across. A perfectly nice chap, but very, very hairy.

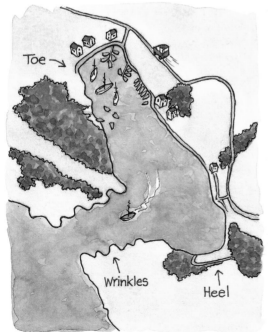

Apart from the top of his head. This man was a walking scribble. He had long wispy curly black hair all over his face, back, shoulders, arms, legs and probably... I don't want to think about that any more.

I suppose he should be a Cruising Character but I'd rather not draw him now if you don't mind. It was bad enough with that hairy Italian footballer we met in the last book. But don't let me put you off Porto Koufo though; Mr Scribble's probably not there any more.

Oh alright then, I'll draw him.

Well, I did warn you.

The rest of Halkidiki's middle finger was pleasant enough but like the first was mainly given over to disco beaches and holidaymakers. Jetskis buzzed around aimlessly like flies on a window. No place for a yacht to want to anchor. I guess we're more than a little spoilt. Once you've dropped the hook in a secluded bay and jumped over the side for a swim, climbing back up to dry off in the sun on deck, put the kettle on, open a bottle, nibble some olives, why would you want to go and lie on a beach all day? Particularly with a couple of thousand decibels of europop blasting the skin off your eardrums.

Maybe I *am* getting old. Nobody plays nice gentle music with jolly tunes any more like, you know, Cream or Hendrix or ZZ Top or Motörhead. It's sad really.

The monks and the mountain

The most interesting of the three fingers is the one that's the most difficult to visit. Mount Athos, or the Akti peninsula, is a self-governing state within Greece, run by its 20 Eastern Orthodox monasteries. Greece's answer to the Vatican, but without the tax-free $10-15 billion in the coffers. Despite that the monasteries appeared to be thriving. Of the dozen or so we sailed past, all had a tower crane or two. The whole place was expanding, it seemed. There was a sense of continuous growth. Scattered all along the coast were smaller settlements, some just a privy-sized hut. A cluster of privies was overshadowed by an outhouse. A

group of outhouses by a chapel, all set to grow into a mini monastery, no doubt planning its very own tower crane. It was as if religion was an underground mycelium penetrating the rock, forever spawning new mushroom growth above ground. Although it's not an island you can only visit by boat. You apply for a permit in advance approved by four leading monasteries. If you're female, forget it, unless you're a convincing male impersonator. Apparently the monks believe that the presence of women alter the social dynamics of a community. Can't argue with that. It used to be that female animals were also excluded from the peninsula. I'm still working on that one.

Some female Euro MPs (and a couple of nanny goats) have grumbled that this contravenes the intention of the Schengen Agreement to remove border controls and allow free movement to all. The response of the Autonomous Monastic State of the Holy Mountain was that the agreement was Satanic, and what was worse, some of the numbers used in the Agreement's passport database contained the number 666, which of course is the Number of the Beast. Don't know why you Euro MPs hadn't thought of that one.

Seeing Mount Athos for the first time you realise why the monks are there. The Holy Mountain is an enormous dramatic imposing huge whacking great chunk of limestone rising steeply to 2033 metres, out at the end of the peninsula. If those monks don't find God there I don't know where he is. On the tip of the peninsula, the buildings dwindled to shelters again, clinging to the southern slopes, forever looking out to sea. Mount Athos slowly shrank away as we sailed on a bouncy broad reach to the island of Limnos, next stop on our way to Istanbul. Or so we thought…

Mediterranean wildlife

So while we're bouncing our way to Limnos why don't you have a look at some of the creatures you might encounter as you bounce *your* way through the Med.

In the air

The ubiquitous Cooper's Shitehawk strongly resembles the Mediterranean Gull.

In the boat, if you don't watch out

It's only the female mozzie that causes the problem for us, needing copious amounts of blood before she can produce any eggs, as shown here. The male is a veggie, happy with plant juice and nectar and probably an inoffensive sort of chap. Bit of a hippy really.

And however hard you try, eventually you'll get cockroaches on your boat, if only one or two. They come in as eggs in corrugated cardboard boxes. Don't let them on board! But then some roaches can fly. Some can swim. And they can all walk along your mooring lines.

In *Pets on board* I've suggested accepting them as low-maintenance pets but if that doesn't do it for you, at least buy them these little houses with sticky floors so that they can expire in the privacy of their own homes.

Sticky stuff

Here's something else that can walk along your mooring lines. Ratty. You can put rat barriers made from old water bottles on your lines if you like. It will stop all but the Giant Leaping Rats of Santorini. But don't get paranoid; in five years cruising we've never seen a single one.

Aaaarrgh!!! What's that big brown furry thing just under your stomach!? What? Oh. Well, put your clothes on at once.

On the land

Goats are everywhere in Greece. To anchor in a quiet bay, and hear the faint tinkling of bells, then to look up to see them streaming down a hillside is part of the Greek experience, and probably funded by the Greek Tourist Board. But they do eat absolutely everything. This black and white goat was munching leaves on a black and white tree in the superbly sheltered Monastery Bay, Panormitis, on the island of Simi.

Mediterranean dogs are lively, alert and energetic.

And so are the cats.

In the water

If we didn't have dolphins, we'd have to invent them. When you're on a passage and you reach one of those points where you get pissed off with it all - maybe it's threatening rain, or the wind's all over the place, or you're just bored - up come the dolphins like some mad energetic aquatic dance troupe, and proceed to use your bow wave to surf, leap, twist in the air, belly flop, and generally show off. Often they turn to look at you as if to say 'Whoopee! Look at me!' Then after ten minutes or so they all decide that the show is over. One or two may make a curtain call, then they're off. And you're left with a big grin on your face. Never fails.

There are plenty of turtles lurking in Turkey, but they are wary. This may be all you see of the Turkish Lurking Turtle.

64

At the Dokou Strait near Ermione, just round the corner from Poros, the fast current attracts a lot of fish. As we entered we saw a commotion in the water behind us, and gulls wheeling and diving above it. Then a whiskered face surfaced and peered at us.

It was either a monk seal or Lennie Henry doing his David Bellamy impression (I think they're both endangered species). He rolled on his back clutching a fine fish and proceeded to chew its head off, looking very pleased with himself. So we're still not sure.

Do fish dream of mortality? I wondered whether sardines ever come across tins like this and go all cold.

And who knows what else is lurking in the depths?

Oh no, it's that bloody octopus again off the front cover.

Not **Sailing to Byzantium**

We bounced into Myrina harbour on Limnos. So far so good. Our plan was to sail from there to the Turkish island of Gökçeada (never mind that you couldn't clear Customs there - we'd blag our way through wouldn't we?) Then pootle up the Dardanelles to Istanbul. The Blue Mosque, Hagia Sofia, the Grand Bazaar and all the kebabs you could eat. *Sailing to Byzantium* in fact! What a romantic notion! (William Butler Yeats, eat your heart out. Get back to Innisfree and build your cabin instead of just going on and on about it).

Some Swiss sailors in the harbour told us we'd left it a month too late. They had gone to Istanbul in June before the Meltemi had set in for the summer and were on their way back. We listened politely then went below. 'What do you think?' said Liz. 'Load of old tosh. They're Swiss aren't they? If we'd been talking about mountain goats, yodelling or Toblerone I'd have given them the benefit of the doubt but surely two or three weeks can't make that much difference?'

When we poked our nose round the north coast of Limnos the Meltemi

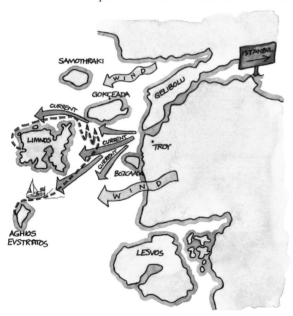

was blasting in from the northeast and the current out of the Dardanelles was in full flow. It was like walking up a very fast 'down' escalator, and after 8 hours of bouncing along under engine at the dizzying speed over ground of 2.5 knots we decided to turn back, let the Meltemi blow itself out in a day or so, and try again later. As we turned I thought I heard a faint sound of yodelling above the wind.

We waved to the Swiss as we tied up to the harbour wall for a second night, ready to be off the next morning. For the next eight days the Meltemi howled and howled. It didn't let up for a minute. We were going nowhere. Now Myrina harbour is a lovely place to stay. Sheltered, quiet, friendly, unspoilt, and although we'd paid for the first day on the harbour wall, nobody bothered to come again and take our money. There was water and even shore power after a friendly fisherman lent us an adaptor (try *that* in Mallorca in August). But after eight days we had to make some sort of effort, so off we went. After 10 hours motoring we cleared Limnos's northernmost point. How are we doing then? Speed 2.3 knots. Oh dear.

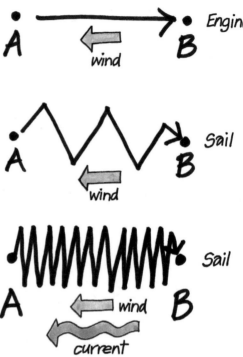

Without the adverse current we should have been able to do the proper sailor's thing and tack our way up to Istanbul (for the nautically-challenged, this means zigzagging your way upwind instead of heading straight into it - you go further and it takes longer but at least you're sailing and not burning diesel). If you've got three or four days to spare to travel a hundred miles in anything between discomfort and abject misery it's well worth doing. But the current made that impossible. With Yanina's modest rig and that current we'd have tacked all the way back to Levkas.

No, we now had a different choice. Going back to Limnos was out of the question, simply on the basis of self-respect. Imagine skulking back into harbour for another week or so, facing the grins on the fishermen's faces (at least the Swiss had gone, off on a downwind jaunt to the Cyclades, the smartypants). No, couldn't do it. So our choice was to grit our teeth, thrash the engine and arrive in Istanbul some time just after Christmas, or turn right and go south-east, and at least we could sail on something like a beam reach (at right-angles to the wind - much easier) and surely we could make Lesvos? Must be possible.

If you hold a powerful magnifying glass up to the chart, you can see a tiny speck of an island south of Limnos called Ayios Evstratios. I don't think it figures in any tourist brochure or many guidebooks but it's there, and that's where we could end up if we didn't go for Istanbul and if we couldn't reach Lesvos. Clinging to a minute Greek rock in the middle of nowhere.

It was then, pondering this, that nearly two weeks' worth of frustration welled up, and Liz, standing at the wheel, shouted, 'Are we wimps or what? We're going to Istanbul!'

It is moments like this that bring into focus the fact that your future life is laid out ahead of you by random elements out of your control - call it chance, co-incidence, a sequence of chaos-based inter-related meteorological micro-events originally caused by the missed beat of a butterfly's wing in Guatemala or just a ripple in the entropy flow of the universe. Because a nanosecond after Liz uttered the syllable '-bul' a rogue wave that had begun its journey somewhere to the west of Samothraki island just happened to jostle a Turkish rogue wave that hailed from Bozcaada near the mainland. The second rogue picked up the first and flung

it, a big glassy green lump of salty water, right on top of her.

As the cockpit drains gurgled, there was a moment's silence in the maelstrom. Turning the wheel to starboard, she said, 'Alright, we'll get the bus.'

Stale bread and quasimodogs

After a few hours of bucking, rolling, tipping, cursing, swearing and generally whinging and grumbling, we found the end of the harbour wall at Ayios Evstratios, and turned the corner into calm, calm, calm. It never ceases to amaze me how hiding behind big lumps of concrete and stone can change your quality of life so much. We tied up alongside behind the two big fishing boats that were also sheltering there. So it wasn't just us.

Everyone in Ayios Evstratios lived in the same village, its arms wrapped around the harbour. There was little else on the island except some sheep, goats, a cemetery, a rubbish tip, and the rusted remains of a wind turbine up on the hill, that looks as if it was blown down some time in the 1970s. The baker must have died years ago, because the only bread came by ferry every other day from Limnos and it was always a day old. But there were a couple of pleasant bars and tavernas.

And where there are fishing boats there are fish. A fisherman came up to us and pointed at our water hose. Borrow? he signed. Of course, we signed back. He didn't speak Greek or English. He was Egyptian. We lent him the hose. Back it came an hour later along with a bag full of lovely big fish, more than we could eat in a week. What do you do with that lot when you've no freezer on board? Well, you take it all to the taverna, offer it as a gift to the cook, and ask her to grill your choice of fish that evening for free. That's how it works here.

The other thing the island specialised in was a spectacularly ugly, determinedly scruffy dog with cross eyes and a pronounced overbite. I guess canine one-night stands must have taken place for so long they're a breed of their own, and would certainly won the Best Degenerate of Show at the Greek version of Cruft's. I'm going to claim it as a breed when I get round to it, and call it the Quasimodog.

A Farewell to Hams?

The Coast Guard finally kicked us out of Ayios, and we made our way east to Lesvos, home of the Lesvians (that's how the Greeks spell it, not me). It's remarkable how one dead female Greek poet and a few lines in a slim volume can lead to a whole radical social sexual and political lifestyle being named after her birthplace. Would you call the Liberal party the Llanystumdwians because Lloyd George came from a small village in North Wales?

Lesvos has its cute, pretty touristy villages in the usual over-sweet way the Greeks do so well. But being so close to Turkey, the island has its own character, and also its own garrison of soldiers. After all this is the eastern limit of the EU and the western world. Turkey is the beginning of the Levant. Go ashore here and you can get a bus straight to Damascus.

So they're all a bit touchy about the border, and from Lesvos you will be tracked by the Coast Guard's radar. So you can't just wander from Greek island to Turkish mainland and back willy-nilly, much as it may be fun to do so. You have to clear Greek customs to leave Greece, and do the same on entering Turkey. And the process there takes the best part of a day and costs about 30 euros. So you don't want to have to go through that every other day, do you?

Well, you soon find out that things aren't actually that bad. It's only on Lesvos and some of the bigger islands further south where the radar noses after you. Elsewhere, if you're unscrupulous, you can shuttle back and forth from Turkish mainland to Greek island whenever you feel the need for a pork souvlaki

71

and a Greek salad. Just don't wave a toy camel or a fez around in the Greek harbours. We know a couple who did just this all the way down to Bodrum (not the toy camel and fez bit). They'd written a book too. Spooky eh?

But all this was future knowledge to us as we sailed east to Turkey, the Meltemi raging well to the west, and we entered the miniature archipelago that marks the entrance to Ayvalik, at the northern end of the Turkish coast. And what's more, a large friendly well-run marina, set in a big noisy bustling town with crowded streets, traffic, bars, shops, and 'Alahu Akbar' wafting from the pencil slim towers of mosques. And everywhere, from hill tops to school buildings, huge scarlet flags and pictures of Kemal Atatürk, founder of modern Turkey, Big Daddy-in-Chief, and in a land where to deny yourself alcohol is the official norm, probably the only Turk who could have drunk George Best under the table. After years of abuse, Atatürk's liver finally gave up the ghost in 1938 and no-one's been able to match him since.

Except maybe Oliver Reed. Ollie would probably have arm-wrestled him too.

Talking Turkey

When you get to Turkey the muezzin's wailing plaintive call to prayer to the faithful will be the loudest Turkish voice you will hear. The rest of them are polite, charming, friendly and courteous, and speak a language that is unlike anything you will have heard so far in the Med. Even Greek. And they have some great words: it's a smutty schoolboy's delight.

Do you remember those rainy lunchtimes at school when, to relieve the boredom you and your mates went into the library to look up rude words in the big blue Oxford Dictionary, sniggering over the results? No? Really? Oh. It's just me then.

Anyway, the Turkish language and manners must have come over from the Asian steppes with Genghis Khan and his Tartar hordes ('Good evening everyone, no need to panic. My name's Genghis and these are my hordes. I've come to invade you. Those of you who want to be pillaged move over to the left; the rest follow me.') The Turks are so friendly and polite I'm sure that's how he would have said it.

Wherever it came from the language must be difficult to translate. Just look at this restaurant sign. The unsuspecting waiter clearly confused his tentacles with his testicles.

Turkish baths.
In the sea.

Just down from Ayvalik is Bademli Limani (which translates as 'Almond Harbour'), a shallow silted-up bay, protected by two islands between which is a wonderful sheltered anchorage. On the shoreline was a small outdoor hamam, built over an outflow of hot fresh water. A few yards away was a Jacuzzi-sized stone bath with fresh water bubbling up from the bottom, in which an elderly woman and her daughter were washing clothes in it. 'Welcome to Turkey', they said, and smiled. Behind the trees above the shore were families camping, cooking, sleeping on the grass. It was a peaceful sort of place. And we did what the *Turkish Waters Pilot* suggested. We sat in the hot tub and watched the sun set over the islands.

Next morning gave us our first experiences of Turkish hospitality to strangers. Walking to Bademli town, we stopped for coffee and our money was waved away. Five minutes later we tried to buy some tomatoes from an old man sitting outside his tiny fruit and veg shop. He didn't have enough small change, so he pressed the tomatoes into our hands (fortunately he didn't press too hard) and waved our money away.

In town the faithful had overflowed the mosque onto the pavement to kneel in prayer. A young man talked into his mobile nearby while they prayed. All very relaxed. We left money for the fruit and veg man, presumably now at prayer, and walked back past a ramshackle one-storey stone hovel with a patched-up tin roof. Sprouting two or three satellite dishes. I hope having 300 TV channels won't change their traditional values.

The quiet coast:
unreconstructed notes straight from my notebook

Crossed to Eski Foça, two dolphins played around us, both with scratches on their backs. From fights?

Flat calm: gulls sitting spaced apart. As they take off, without any wind to give them a lift, they push with their feet on the water.

Eski Foça: small but lively Turkish holiday resort. Anchored across the bay. Dinghy across to see if it's a place we can busk. Music festival. Live band in park. Big video screen. On N quay small band with an eclectic mix of instruments setting up to play for free in the street. We go back to eat on board, come back later to miss them. Carpe Diem!!

In morning wander round, ask way from waiter. Invites us for coffee, sits, chats, declines our offer to pay. Give him card. Anchorages: Hoteleran and Sarpdere. Rod's 'breathtaking beauty'. Fish farms everywhere.

Sigacik, small low-key marina, walled town, people living as they would have done for centuries. We walk through the village at dusk saying 'Iyi akşamlar' and watching wary faces break into smiles. Restaurant run by Jacques le Marseillais. Mezze plate, seabass, prawns in garlic & chili, fennel, rocket. £35. Best meal for months? 2 years? Mixed fruit on the house. Joined Nusret, the marina manager, & ma & Dutch couple for coffee. Head waiter & boys, Jacques' boozer's nose.

Entire building covered in varnished pebbles inside and out. Like being in an aquarium.

In the morning the muezzin wails in F#. A tiny kitten fearlessly walking, jumping, half-climbing up the kerb to the fish stalls for breakfast, walking undaunted among the heedless boys' feet. Take the dolmus to Seferihisar (tangerines and satsumas) quiet town. Street of doctors, street of plastic hosepipe, street of plastic washing up bowls. Bread in glass cases delivered by baker every a.m. Ruined hammam, washing hanging up round it. Line of tree-covered cafés, all full of men playing backgammon and cards. MDF chests, bookends, letter racks, vases, cabinets. Rod's 'hinterland'. Chair with no back leg leaning on wall outside shop. Woman sitting (sensibly) on pavement next to it.

Waiters carrying trays of tea in glasses acros the road. Glass eye set in the floor at the threshhold of a clothes shop.

30 miles across to Kusadasi. No wind again.

Kusadasi

After Turkey's quiet coast Kusadasi is a bit of a shock. It's the cruise ships' nearest stop for Ephesus, Turkey's blockbuster of an ancient ruined city, and it's one big bazaar. The Kapali Carsi, the covered market, has overflowed into the streets around it, with signs for 'Genuine fake watches' and stallholders calling 'Eenglish? I love Eenglish money' and 'Hello, how can I take your money?' (refreshingly honest that one). It's fun for a while.

The Turkish barber

In Kusadasi I ventured into my first Turkish barber shop for a simple haircut, not knowing that there is no such thing in the Turkish barber's selection of services. They will cut, trim, shave, scrape, and massage just about anything you point towards them.

This one listened attentively to my request in broken (shattered?) Turklish for a little bit off the sides, leave it resting on the ears, a bit more off the top but not so it sticks up like a coconut, not too much off the back, etc, etc. Twenty minutes later I got what everybody gets: the standard Turkish man's haircut, short, neat, and in my case sticky-up on the top, which Liz calls my 'toilet brush look'.

But he'd only just got started. My shoulders were shaved down as far as he could stretch the neck hole in my T-shirt without throttling me, my eyebrows trimmed down to a bristly stubble, my nostril hair eradicated for a good foot up my nasal passages. I declined the offer of a shave with a cut-throat razor. Then came the pièce de résistance. A thin stick was dipped in meths, lit, and whacked against each ear for an instant to singe the bristly hairs therein but presumably not set the earwax alight. Jets of flame coming out the ears? No thanks. Finally a cotton wool ball was rapidly inserted into each ear and just as rapidly whipped out again. All done with skill, energy and panache, and leaving me with a faint smell of charred hair around my lugs and an irresistible desire to run screaming out of the shop.

Me and 'er meandering up the Menderes valley

To escape Kusadasi and its demon barbers, you can get a coach trip to Ephesus, but the best way is to rent a car for a day, go as early as you can, and stay ahead of the crowds and the heat. You won't avoid them altogether, but by the time they catch up you've seen most of the ruined city and imagined how people lived and worked there, and you can be out before lunch. Then you can drive up the valley of the river Menderes*, and see how people live and work today. Field upon field crammed with vegetables and fruit trees stretch away into the distance. The fields are worked by real gypsies, living in real gypsy encampments, as they have for centuries. New Age travellers with piercings, dogs and old Transit vans they most definitely are not.

For a while we drove slowly behind a tractor pulling an open trailer. It was piled high with crates of peaches, with four women standing on the back, chatting

and laughing, as if they were gossiping in the village square. One was peeling peaches and handing them to the others. As she waved her knife around to emphasise a particular point, it flew out of her juice-covered hand and into the road. Screams and shouts and much waving of arms ensued. The driver stopped, the peach peeler jumped off and ran to pick up her knife, flashing a brilliant smile as she passed us. The others pulled her back up, peeling, chatting and laughing was resumed and we were all on our way. It just wouldn't happen on the A34.

Stop off in Sirçe and sample the streets, sorted according to hardware in the traditional way: the Street of a Thousand Saucepans, a Thousand Handbag Makers, there's even a Street of a Thousand Tractor Tyres.

* It's where the verb *To meander* came from

77

You'll be the only Westerner in town so expect to be stared at a little bit - it's only natural curiosity. After all, how would *you* react if a real Westerner, let's say a Texan in a ten-gallon hat, bootlace tie and crocodile skin cowboy boots, turned up in Ramsbottom? Come to think of it, they'd probably never notice. New-fangled notions are afoot in Ramsbottom* as they are everywhere. The Ramsbottomians all go line-dancing for fun and they probably all wear snakeskin boots and bootlace ties instead of clogs and white mufflers.

Driving in the blistering heat we discovered that they have something here that Ramsbottom doesn't have. Filling stations with showers for cars. Not a car wash, but a sensible response to driving all day in temperatures up to 40°C, cooling your car down before you stop to fill up. Made us nostalgic for English drizzle. How very civilised of the Turks to come up with this notion. Well done, lads. Teşekkür ederim (Ta very much) as they say round here.

Further up the river valley, past neat houses with neat tractors parked neatly in front of them, past the wonderfully-named Kuçulukçuk, to Birge. Come here for a glimpse of life in the 19th century Ottoman Empire. Old timber-framed houses crowd each side of the narrow rocky stream, dominated by the restored Merchant's House, a residence with a suite of rooms for each of the owner's wives ('The Stamboul Lady and the Izmir Lady') complete with original wall paintings.

*Locals used to call Ramsbottom 'Tup's Arse' but now they enunciate it as *Rems-bó-tham*. This is a common development in Britain now. Since Burnage, an inner suburb of Manchester, became famous as the home of Oasis's Gallagher brothers, it's original pronunciation of *Bér-nidge* is now the Franco-philic *Bourn-ájhe*, while Stalybridge has just gone all glitzy and is now known universally as Stalyvegas (locals still wear clogs there though I believe they spray them with glitter now). I provide this information for northern yachties who've been away too long.

Paradise gained

Sail southwest from Kusadasi, squeeze your way between Samos and the Turkish mainland, and by the end of the day you can reach Paradise Bay, described in the Pilot book as an 'idyllic anchorage'. Paradise for us meant a fish farm, cloudy water (fish food? fish poo?) and 41°C in the shade, with hot gusty winds coming off the land, but it was still beautiful for all that. In fact down this coast there are dozens of equally beautiful, pine-sheltered, quiet and empty little anchorages. You do get a bit blasé ('I say, darling, is this one more idyllic than the last one or less?' 'Oh slightly less, I'd say. Just not quite perfection.' 'Yes, you're so right. What a damn shame.' 'Oh absolutely.').

Asin, further down the coast, is a tiny ancient harbour with a friendly and welcoming submerged harbour wall lurking at the entrance. We got in without scraping anything, swapped places on the quay with a charter boat and ended up too close to a grumbling fisherman ('Problema problema.') There was room for him really. The boy who took our money for the mooring seemed a bit grumbly and surly too. In fact the whole place seemed a bit grumbly and surly, as if nobody could really be arsed and it was all really too much.

A shame because a stone's throw across the harbour is the ruined remains of Iassos, a 9th century BC Greek city. During the day a man sits at the entrance in his wooden box and takes your money, but wait until he finishes his shift at six and you can stroll in. The heat of the day was almost spent, dusk was imminent, and we shared the place with two donkeys and an artist drawing the agora. What an atmosphere. In the twilight it could have been a set for Midsummer Night's Dream.

By contrast to both Paradise and Asin, our next stop was Yalikavak, then the newest marina in Turkey. Air-conditioned showers, supermarkets, bars, posh restaurants, art exhibitions, a modern amphitheatre with free concerts and traditional Turkish music in the streets. It was utter unashamed self-indulgent luxury. Nice every now and then.

Never go back

We dragged ourselves away from Yalikavak with its locally-owned powerboats registered in Wilmington Delaware, stars and stripes at the stern, and headed for Kalymnos. We'd had an enjoyable backpacking holiday in Kalymnos when we were young and foolish and had met Themis, a restaurant owner who entertained us one night with the jolly story of how his Mercedes was blown up with dynamite nicked from the site for the new airport (just a boyish prank - Greek style). We were curious. Was he still there, grey-haired and fatter now? Did he have a new Merc?

But Kalymnos is in Greece innit? So we checked out of Turkey (didn't we? 'Course we did. Couldn't go hopping between Greece and Turkey without doing that, could we?) and entered Kalymnos harbour, dropped the kedge off the back and tied up bows-to on the wall. Perfect. Unfortunately the wind had other ideas, blowing our stern round and helping our kedge (our old CQR anchor) to plough through the weed on the bottom. We came to a stop alongside the quay, nonchalantly trying to look as if we'd planned it all along.

After two hours in the hot sun searching for Themis's restaurant we just gave up. The place had changed totally. Commercial. Tacky. Touristy. I suppose that's what an airport does for a Greek island. I wandered off looking for a bottle of gas while Liz got back on board. A shout from the quay brought her up on deck, to find a Port Police man telling us to move on.

'You haven't by any chance come from Turkey, have you?' he asked. 'Turkey? Us? Oh no,' replied Liz sweetly and innocently. 'What was your last port?' A pause while Liz thought. 'Erm... just a minute.' She dashed down the companionway and frantically looked on the chart. She dashed back up again.

'Lakki, on Leros,' replied Liz sweetly and innocently. 'And before that?'

'Erm... just a minute.' She dashed down the companionway and frantically looked on the chart. She dashed back up again.

'Agathonisi,' replied Liz sweetly and innocently. This could have gone on all the way back to Malta, but as I'd got back with the gas, our man on the quay must have got bored with the game and just told us to clear off. We were only too happy to oblige.

Never go back, they always say.

The Kaptan, the Turk, his Wife and their Merchant Banker

It was four in the afternoon. We were leaving a safe but unwelcoming Kalymnos harbour and looking for shelter for the night. But where? Eight or ten miles round the headland gets you to a tiny steep-sided harbour called Vathi. There are at least half a dozen Vathis in the Greek islands but this one would do nicely thank you, even though it meant motoring at full cock into the usual Meltemi maelstrom and hot gusty headwinds. Nothing for it but get the sprayhood down, strip down to swimming trunks, thrash the engine and just get splashed with salt spray every

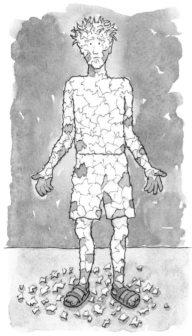

five seconds for three or four hours. As we approached Vathi, the waves got bigger. The wind, hotter than a flying vindaloo, blasted out of the steep-sided tiny cleft in the rock that was the harbour entrance. Once inside, calm, peace, and another exquisite miniature harbour. No weedy bottom, no Port Police, just a handy fish taverna within staggering distance across the quay. By this time the brine on my body had evaporated to an all-over crust, making me feel somewhat like Lot's wife must have felt just after she looked back at Sodom. Is this why Liz often calls me a crusty old sod?

We were on the end of the quay but there was just room for a sizeable power boat, flying the stars and stripes (that'll be Turkish then), to come nosing in next to us. We jumped ashore to take their lines as they carefully nudged their way in, trying not to hit us in the cross-wind.

Though there were three others on deck the Kaptan was anchoring, steering, leaping down to handle the lines, and showing impressive control of the situation. Once tied on, he signed a thank you, dived overboard to check the anchor, then hauled himself back on board. I warmed to him even more when, one finger to his lips, he surreptitiously slid us a bottle of wine for our help.

His passengers were an elderly Turkish couple and their son. In the evening while we got ready to go up to the taverna a few yards away, the son had a discussion with the taverna owner and a table and chairs were brought down and placed in the middle of the quay for the three of them to dine al fresco. Not the Kaptan. No doubt he'd be thrown a few chicken bones afterwards.

The taverna owner, in a kaftan Demis Roussos would have been proud of, fed us goat stew and retsina, and gave us a free melon to finish. Back on board we sat in the cockpit looking at the stars. From the shadows on the power boat a voice said 'Good evening.' It was the son. Parents safely tucked in bed, he was also looking at the stars. We started chatting. He was interested in our lifestyle and asked us searching questions about the whole liveaboard thing. He was the owner of the power boat, taking his parents for a cruise. I asked about his job.

'I'm the CEO of a merchant bank in Istanbul. I show foreign investors the top 100 companies in Turkey and encourage their investment. I studied business management and law in the USA.' We discussed his country. 'When Ataturk built modern Turkey he picked the best from each European country. For example from the French he took the legal code. I know because I'm a lawyer. Turkey looks to Europe for the future.'

I asked about how Ataturk imposed cultural homogeneity by banning Kurdish and gipsy music. 'Is this attitude relaxing now?' 'There are still conservative elements but yes it is, certainly in Istanbul. It's a thriving bustling Western city in the East. I live on the European side in the Genoese-built quarter. But what do you do?' We told him we were designers.

'It must be good making things. I don't make anything.'

'Apart from a profit?'

'It's not enough. I need something more.'

It's true what they say about money.

In the morning at 6.30 I heard goat bells, and poked my head up to see the goatherd and about 50 goats tinkling along the path above the harbour. Turk Senior was on deck having a quiet smoke. 'Good morning. Have you seen our Kaptan? He is missing.'

At that moment his Kaptan emerged from the water, holding up a spear and two fine fish. Useful man, that.

The crinkly bits

East from Kalymnos is the beginning of Turkey's really crinkly baroque bits of coastline. Gökova Körfezi, a gulf stretching almost 50 miles, is guarded on the north by Bodrum. You could spend weeks exploring the coastline between here and Marmaris in the next bay round the Datça Peninsula. As an antidote to busy Bodrum, try Küçük ('Small') bay, a tiny totally sheltered bay. Drop the anchor in the middle and swim ashore with a line to tie round a tree and you're all set. Nobody else there, just a couple of small fishing boats, and through the scrub pine, a fisherman's makeshift shack in a clearing.

Cruising ☺ Characters

Right up into the Gökova Körfezi is Keçi Bükü, Rod Heikell's 'ultimate gem', a superbly sheltered deep bay with a smart marina and a few restaurants with rickety jetties. It was here we met Simon and Orit on Kaulua, a diminutive home-built catamaran. Simon was a spare, gregarious Englishman with a ready smile and beads in his beard. Orit, from Israel, resembled a tiny bird wearing Oakley shades. They met while travelling, and then just carried on, swapping backpacks for a boat. Whenever they needed money they just called Manpower and worked in a factory for a few weeks. They had a flat in Haifa, Israel. Orit's parents went there from Poland in 1958. We swapped books and chatted about their lifestyle. Their home for four years, Kaulua possessed no luxuries. No fridge, no diesel engine. Orit gave us some home-made yoghurt, and told us of the restaurant they had run in Haifa, that did meals only when they managed to get fifteen or so people together. Massage and healing were somehow involved too. A lesson there for our TV chefs, I think.

Heading south we stopped at Knidos, on Cape Deveboynu at the tip of the Datça peninsula. A beautiful anchorage on one side of the isthmus, a perfectly round Roman harbour on the other. Overlooking both were the ruins of a sizeable amphitheatre. Ignore the whistles of the restaurant owners ashore and drop the hook in 12 feet of vodka-clear water. Dinghy to the jetty and wander round the ruins at dusk.

At breakfast the next morning we watched a shoal of tiny silver fish being plundered by pencil-thin trumpetfish (which look nothing like the drawing but I wish they did). Taking turns they would dart into the shoal and emerge with an unlucky wriggling fish in its jaws. We settled for cornflakes.

Building gülets in Bozburun

The crinklier this coastline gets the more little nooks and crannies there are. Bozburun is one such. Tucked right up into the head of a big sheltered bay, it has a small harbour that can only be described as 'cute'. There are plenty of Turkish gülets round here and it's not surprising. They make 'em here, just round the corner. We wandered down, keen to see a real Turkish boatyard.

ʕ The gület

ʕ The workforce   ʕ The workshop

And that's what we found. A yard. Not even a yard, more a corner of a field where three men were slowly putting together 60-foot long wooden boats using just curved metal and wood patterns lying around the yard. A sawbench stood a few yards away, covered in straw against the heat of the sun. And that was it. Computer-aided design? No way. Laser-controlled levelling system? Don't be silly. Epoxy laminate construction? Come off it, mate.

Although there are large yards building high quality supergülets in steel and GRP, here in Bozburun it was all local pine, laid out by eye and hand in the time-honoured method and knocked together with galvanised nails. A yachtie I met had asked one of the builders why they didn't use bronze nails or even copper. 'They'll be back in three years for repairs,' he replied.

Fun with holding tanks

Gollygosh, we're back to talking about toilets again. It is after all the most discussed subject whenever more than one yachtie gets together for more than ten minutes (if you hear of just one yachtie getting together for a chat call for the men in the white coats).

YOU CAN PUT ANYTHING DOWN HERE AS LONG AS YOU EAT IT FIRST

This bit could easily fit elsewhere in this little book but here will do. It runs in nicely with Ken's Holding Tank story which follows. The term 'holding tank' is a bit of a nautical euphemism but let's stick with it.

So what is it? When you pump out the marine toilet (which I introduced to the Dwellers of the Soil amongst you in *On the nose*), you pump it out through a hole in the hull. That's fine at sea, but in an idyllic anchorage with lovely clear water and people swimming up to your boat asking where Bosham is, it's not so good. So that which must be pumped out must be held in your tank for a few days until you can get clear of land and get shut of it.

Many countries are very concerned about the whole issue and will fine you thousands of euros or dollars if you are caught polluting the sea nearer than several miles offshore. In the Med it's particularly Turkey with its beautifully clear water that is concerned about this, but other countries are catching up.

Turkish Coast Guard helicopters patrol the coastline and the marinas regularly and anyone caught pumping out where they shouldn't will be in deep do -do. Spending a penny round here might cost you a 10,000 euro fine. In Marmaris Yat Marine the water was so clean there was a swimming area *in the marina.* Unthinkable in Spain.

So unless you have a porta-potty from your old caravan, you have to install the holding euphemism thingy. And what a fun job it is. I did ours in Malta ready for our trip to Turkey. It's not difficult but it involved drilling yet more holes in the boat's hull and, as in all boat jobs, I needed to be a four-foot high contortionist with three telescopic arms, scratchproof magnetic fingers and X-ray eyes to do it properly. I put in a diverter valve to pump directly out at sea, but switch to the tank at anchor. Other people bung it all through the tank, then out. It's up to you. I also had a valve leading up to a deck fitting in the extremely unlikely event of getting to anywhere that had a pump-out facility. Before you start to gnaw your knuckles in boredom, this all means that there are a lot of big inch-and-a-half diameter plastic pipes snaking their way round the heads…

… like this. I like to think it's the marine toilet equivalent of Piano & Rogers' Pompidou Centre at Beaubourg in Paris. They won architectural prizes for sticking all the plumbing on the outside of the walls so why shouldn't I? And it's easier when the pipes need cleaning out (which they do, no matter how much malt vinegar some American internet toilet guru tells you to pour down the pan). You see, they eventually get clogged up with calcium deposits, like giant furred arteries that you get from eating too many chip butties. Malt vinegar just isn't man enough to unblock them, and you need to bash them on the marina pontoon every now and then to break the deposits out. On some boats these can be very long pipes. A friend of ours who shall remain nameless* had this problem. He plugged both ends of a 14-foot length of pipe, gingerly carried it out to the pontoon, grabbed one end and gave it a mighty swing down onto the pontoon, forgetting about the bung in the end. Unfortunately, on the next pontoon an unsuspecting French sailor had just put on a nice clean stripey T-shirt and white shorts. Tut tut. Oh dear. Quel dommage. Tant pis.

*What the hell, it was Nige and Al on Strummer. They're half way round the world now, they won't mind me telling.

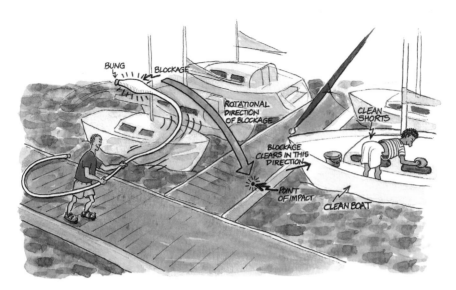

But what about your seacocks? Well, you need something stronger than malt vinegar. And in Spanish supermarkets you can buy it. Aguafuerte. 25% hydrochloric acid. Any eight-year-old can wander into a supermercado, drop some acid into his basket, and receive a smile and an 'Aaah, bless the little one!' from the checkout girl. And it does shift the stuff from your seacocks, but don't soak plastic valves for too long or they'll disintegrate. I'd say it's almost as powerful as neat Coca Cola, which the super-mercado can also supply to little Pedro ('Aaah, bless!').

A dangerous couple

But don't store it anywhere near bleach because mixed together they produce chlorine gas, which will rot your skin and eyes, and eventually kill you. There are enough ways to die on a boat without that, thank you.

87

Ken's holding tank story

You just couldn't make this up. Anchored overnight outside a marina, Ken and Alicia were to be hauled out of the water the next day. They had planned to nip out of the bay in the morning to empty their holding tank, but they were called in too early. Only later on in the boatyard did they remember the full tank.

Surrounded by other boats with owners sleeping on board at night, how could they empty it without embarrassment? Ken had a cunning plan. At dead of night he would tiptoe out, hold a bucket under the tank outlet, and quietly tap on the hull as a signal for Alicia to start or to stop pumping. Good plan. Simple and discreet. That night, holding his bucket up, Ken tapped on the hull. Alicia pumped. The bucket filled and got heavier. It suddenly dawned on Ken that he needed two hands to hold it up, leaving no hands to tap on the hull. Oh shit, thought Ken, somewhat appropriately. He tried lifting a leg to kick the hull but had never been able to do the splits. 'Alicia!' hissed Ken, not wanting to wake the neighbours. 'Alicia!!' in a louder hiss this time. 'Al-eeeeeeeeee-cia!!!' Alicia stalwartly carried on pumping. Across the bay in the town's noisy bars and discos, over the insistent and decibel-crammed beat of house and hip-hop could be heard a faint but distinct cry: 'ALICIA FOR F*#K'S SAKE STOP PUMPING!!!!'

Inside the boat Alicia thought she heard something. She went up on deck only to see faces peering down from the surrounding boats at red-faced Ken and his overflowing bucket. 'I s'pose I'll go and empty it then.' said Ken.

88

Now is the winter of our disco tent

We knew we wanted to stay over winter in Marmaris Yat Marine just from talking to other yachties around the Med. Why? The shelter? The facilities? The ambience?

It was cheap, that's why. And it did give remarkable value for money. In the huge boatyard, businesses vied to solve your every problem. There was a superb restaurant with knock-down prices, and a swimming pool right by it. There were showers with air-conditioning and piped music. There was a disco but it wasn't in a tent - I said that just to make Shakespeare spin in his grave.

There were scores of yachties to generally have a good time with over the winter months. And the musical talent! Phil, a brilliant keyboard player and karaoke star, Thomas with his gravelly voice and his endless German folk dirges, a choice of two ex-pro drummers, a professional girl singer, a bass player who'd played with Sting. And me: skilled interpreter of Little Richard's tender love songs. A band just had to be born.

Phil used his management skills as an ex-Army Officer to turn this bunch of middle-aged musos into a band that held together just long enough to do three brilliant gigs before artistic differences and bruised egos, but mainly unfinished boat jobs, took their toll.

Even the girls from the office did their bit dancing on stage.

Although Liz and I missed Christmas at Yat Marine, we were told how Kevin, one of our drummers, had used his formidable interpersonal skills to advantage when he took on the role of Santa for some of the less shy and retiring children.

How many camels?

Mr Aziz, the head waiter in the restaurant, was quite simply besotted with Liz's blonde hair and blue eyes. He was a nice man, married with a tiny baby, so I didn't really mind. As soon as we arrived at the restaurant he would look across the tables with a mournful expression, and find an excuse to come and say hello and gaze into her eyes. Liz of course loved getting more attention than I've given her for the last 20 years. It went on for weeks. One evening I went to the cashier to pay for our meal to find Aziz Bey standing there. I decided we would have to talk man to man.

'Look Aziz old chap, I'll tell you what. 20,000 lira in cash and six camels and she's yours.'

'OK but you must take my wife in exchange.'

I considered this generous offer, but before I could quibble about the baby, the cashier said to me: 'Ha! Six camels? No, no, no. Listen to me. You should ask for more like six hundred at least. My uncle paid 200 for his woman and she *looked* like a camel.'

I got back to the table.

'What were you talking about? Have you paid the bill?' asked Liz.

'Well, yes I did, but strangely enough the cashier gave *me* a tip.'

The net, the fox and the parrot

I mentioned the VHF radio earlier on, and in most marinas there is a Net each morning. At an agreed time a Net Controller will open up discussion, news, call for a weather forecast, and invite everyone to offer up their 'Treasures of the bilge' for sale. It's a useful exchange of news and information. If you want to borrow a tool, say, just go on and ask. The controller will repeat your request, and somebody will be sure to have what you need.

One Net Controller, let's call her Sandra, who had a perfect Radio 4 'cut glass' accent, received a request for a power sander, and repeated it:

'Right, so Dave wants to borrow a power sander to do his woodwork. Otherwise he's faced with a long slow hand-job.'

The few seconds of VHF silence that followed seemed palpable.

In Marmaris, the redoubtable and reliable Foxy always gave the weather forecast. And he gave it his all. By this time wi-fi was around in most marinas, so Foxy could check half a dozen websites and prepare an incredibly thorough forecast including wind, rain, wave heights and direction, humidity, sunrise and sunset, moonrise and moonset, phases of the moon, the lot.

This contrasted to our first winter in the Med. To pick up Radio Monaco, John would string a wire aerial up along the ceiling from his Sony shortwave radio. With his classic BBC accent he'd then read out a very authoritative weather forecast covering the whole of the western Med. When anybody congratulated him on the forecast he would modestly say:

'I am simply the parrot of Monaco.'

He only admitted later that whenever he couldn't tune in to Monaco, he'd make it all up.

The Parrot of Monaco

Of course you didn't *have* to rely on Foxy, or John the Parrot of Monaco. You could get your own. There were excellent forecasting services from all the Mediterranean countries on many radio frequencies, but for a daysail it's VHF radio that's most useful, and each country has its own approach to forecasting.

I'm told the Spanish were great admirers of the Met Office and they initially brought over an English forecaster, but it didn't work out. The climate didn't agree with him.

So how did the other countries do it?

Weather, 'tis nobler in the mind

The Italians used one VHF channel for a continuous 24-hour forecast, using a recorded male voice electronically stitched together word by word. The deep voice and languid Italian intonation imparted a dramatic, even romantic, touch to words like *molto nuvoloso* (cloudy) or *temporali* (thunderstorms). Some words must have worn out from repeated use because here and there a lighter, younger and slightly petulant voice cut in to fill the gaps. The overall effect was that of Dolce and Gabbana locked in a small room constantly interrupting each other. Maybe that's how they work designing all their bling anyway.

Greek forecasts were different. A husky, rather sexy Melina Mercouri-like voice skipped through the forecast. We listened carefully, not knowing the Greeks pronounced '*mp*' as '*b*'. So when, through a haze of static, for the first time we half-heard 'Melina' say 'Thees ees Olybia Rà-dio, Olybia Rà-dio', Liz said 'What's she saying? Libya Radio?' 'No. Wouldn't be in English.' 'Lobia? Lubia?' 'Where's Lubia? Must be something else.' My imagination ran wild. Then it leapt into the air, howled and fell to the ground panting.

But there are other more traditional ways to determine the weather. In the Aegean, locals know there is going to be a Meltemi blowing soon when they see a cigar-shaped cloud hovering over a hill or mountain.

When the moon holds water

As I write this I read that a moon probe has just discovered that the moon does indeed hold water. Not a lot of it, about a US quart in every ton of moon rock according to Jessica Sunshine (are they kidding?) of the University of Maryland. No marinas yet then.

But what I'm talking about is the traditional view that if the new crescent moon appears tilted as in the illustration, it will hold water. That means the month will be dry. However if its tilt looks as if the water will pour out, it'll rain. On the other hand, to some that means 'dry' because the water has poured out already. So does the theory hold water? Well they say it never rains but it pours. So who knows? I don't, I specialise in dry humour.

What may be a little more reliable is the ancient Coptic Storm Calendar, clearly based on serious observation and correlation going on for hundreds if not thousands of years. There's mention of the calendar in the *Mediterranean Cruising Handbook*, and I found reference to the calendar on two websites, from Cyprus and Egypt. All the storms more or less correlate, though with different wind directions. It's plausible. But you might just as well say 'It'll be pretty windy every week or two this winter' and you'd be about right.

More homework needed, Cooper. Go and stand outside the headmaster's office.

M is for...

One thing we learned in Turkey was that while Turkish people are kind and generous, business is business. The first price is never the real price, and if you're buying anything, never was *emptor* more *caveat*. Oh and don't worry about the red tape. Money talks. Here are some examples.

... Meatballs

Having learnt how to bargain in the bazaar at Kusadasi where all the cruise ships dock, we thought we would easily be a match for the chandlers in Marmaris town. The first one gave us a 10% discount straight away so we pushed our luck and asked for more. His head tilted back, his eyebrows raised and his hands spread open.

'In Turkey we have a saying: "How much money, how many meatballs?" '

That'll be a no then.

... Marina, Mayor and Machismo

Turkey has planning issues just like any other country. We were told about one marina where the local council sent in a JCB to knock down the sea wall because it didn't have planning permission, and at the same time red plastic tape was stretched along walls and across doors and windows of most of the marina buildings. The marina owner had correctly applied for planning permission for his buildings, but the approval process, as everyone knew, took years. The owner put the buildings up anyway because, he reasoned, although the council hadn't given permission, they hadn't actually refused, which I think is a delight of Turkish logic. Whatever it is it allowed him to give himself the all-clear.

('So my friend, is it OK if I just put up this office, restaurant, swimming pool, chandlery, minimarket, workshops, toilets and showers and laundry then?' 'Certainly, me old mate, you go right ahead.' 'That's very understanding of you, old chum.' 'Not at all, anything to oblige.')

The mayor had different views of course. The sea wall, which had sensibly been built to protect the road and of course the marina, was deemed illegal, so the mayor decided to act decisively and with vigour, and sent a JCB round to do to it what JCBs do best, as a visible demonstration of the Council's authority. The buildings were all deemed illegal too but they did house people, businesses and stock, hence the use of red tape rather than the JCB.

And finally the mayor owned four hotels so he was probably jealous. It was all a bit of willy-waving, as a friend of mine would say. So what could overcome this obstacle to progress? What could clear a way through this impasse?

Oh yes, I forgot. M is for…

… Money

Money changed hands, JCBs were withdrawn, tape was removed. This is of course all hearsay and probably some way off the truth, but as with all the best rumours I told it all anyway to Eunice, who ran a hamam in downtown Marmaris and was sorting out my bad back at the time. She was able to top the story immediately.

A hotel had been built in a nearby town but the builder hadn't crossed his i's and dotted his t's on the planning paperwork. The council decided to act decisively and with vigour and sent in the JCBs to knock the hotel down. The developer equally decisively and with just as much vigour took the Council to court. The Council lost and had to rebuild the hotel two months later. This bankrupted the Council. It's just good old Mediterranean machismo at work.

Fairy towers and frescos

Gripping as life is in a Turkish marina, you really should get out more. And explore. By bus. Not the local dolmuş, but the big cümfybuş that takes you long distances overnight in reasonable comfort. 13 hours will get you to Cappadocia. Don't miss it - it's remarkable. They filmed bits of Star Wars there and you can understand why. It's other-worldly - like nowhere else you've ever seen. Clusters of 'fairy towers' looking like tall slim mushrooms, the result of erosion of a layer of soft volcanic rock capped by a harder layer. The small town of Goreme, with its bus station (you can get a bus to Damascus from here), cafés with furled umbrellas looking like miniature fairy towers, cave houses and *pansiyons* has grown up in the midst of this landscape. Everywhere there are complete cruciform churches carved out of the rock, their Eastern Orthodox interiors painted with frescos, colours still fresh. As this sign suggested.

Not too far away you can see entire underground 'cities' hacked out of the same rock, where, in times of danger, the locals, their cows, sheep, goats and chickens, could just disappear into the ground like meerkats and stay for weeks or months living life as normal. Up to ten levels below ground would contain dwellings with all mod cons, a church, a school, a winery, a grain store and stables. Ventilation was by a system of chimneys, and wells provided water. We did a little tour that included a visit to an underground city, although really it was more the size of a village. Our enthusiastic tour guide was a little too didactic in her approach to being a tour guide ('Now who can tell me how many levels there are in the city?'

We all shuffled a bit. 'Ten, miss,' mumbled a 54-year-old schoolboy. 'Very good, very good.') but she came unstuck somewhat when off-patter.

'How long did they stay down here?' asked someone. 'The 7th century,' she replied without hesitation. Puzzled looks all round. More shuffling. I found this stuff fascinating though, having been brought up in a damp country by a father who ran a plumbing business and who built his own house. When I was a sprog there seemed to be a constant battle against water; when I went out as a lad with my dad's plumbers we were mending gutters and leaky pipes, looking for rising damp, clearing blocked drains or keeping the rain out of the roof. Water was the eternal enemy. Keeping it out or keeping it in. A bit like a boat really. Then you come to Turkey and find a place that's so dry that people can live quite happily a hundred feet underground for months.

And it *was* dry at Goreme. The air was dry and still too. And that's where you get balloons. We woke early in our rented room to hear the stillness and silence punctuated by soft muffled roars, as if a family of giant cats were purring outside. When I pulled the curtain this is what I saw…

They say it's the only way to fly but I think that's just a load of hot air. You've got to be a basket case to go up in one of those.

Dog days in Pammukale

On the overnight bus back to Marmaris you just have time to break your journey at Pammukale, another unique bit of Turkey. It's a 2-for-1offer when lumped together with Hierapolis, the remains of a Graeco-Roman spa town, but if you're quick about it you can just about whizz round in a morning, before getting the afternoon bus back to the fleshpots of Marmaris.

Hot springs at the top of a hill have created brilliant white limestone terraces like a series of giant overlapping saucers. You used to be able to paddle in them, but no longer, since too many tourists were peeing in the pools. You can now only wander round and look, and watch the local feral dog pack splash about and pee in the pools instead. Nobody told them off while we were there, but then they were locals after all.

Getting the bus to Byzantium

Remember Liz's resigned comment just off the north coast of Limnos? Well, we did get the overnight cümfybuş to Istanbul. My recollection of the trip was a series of stops in big modern towns and cities, with traffic, ring roads, advertising hoardings, lights, and people. Lots of people, lots of bustle, life and energy. If this lot get into the EU we're stuffed. It wasn't the rural backwater of the Menderes valley or the bucolic Turkey of my memories from 30-odd years ago. After an early morning ferry crossing we reached the outskirts of Istanbul, a huge area of squatters' shacks. The Turks call them *gecekondu* (built at night). This city is BIG, almost twice as many people as in London, and getting bigger every day.

At the bus terminus we transferred our bags to a local bus. I say 'we' but we didn't have any say in the matter. A freelance porter leapt on our pile of bags and hoisted them all at once onto various parts of his anatomy. He staggered 25 feet, dropped them on the ground in front of an empty dolmuş, and held his hand out, saying, 'Baksheesh.' I don't know what the going rate is for watching someone lift weights while staggering but it was sort of entertaining so we haggled a bit and paid. After half an hour's waiting we were told it was the wrong

bus. We found the right bus and started off. After 500 yards the bus stopped in the mother of all traffic jams. Horns were blaring, drivers were cursing, cars were reversing down a slip road to find a different way to enter the gridlock. This was it. We'd be stuck here for the next ten years at least. But 40 minutes later we were on our way to our hostel, just down from the Blue Mosque. I'm not going to give you a run down of the tourist attractions in Istanbul; go and buy the Rough Planet. But I did notice a few things worth mentioning. The Topkapi Palace for example. It's enormous, but we could only find one loo. Yet the Sultan had 500 women in there. Can you imagine the queue?

There is plenty to see just wandering round the city. Walk down the hill to the ferry terminal and you go with the flow of the crowd through the rag trade district, shop after shop of identical long grey coats and headscarves as worn by 99% of Turkish women, interspersed with just as many shops displaying a surprising variety of racy underwear. Draw your own conclusions.

At the foot of the hill you reach the spice market, but then your nose told you that half way down.

Give us a whirl

We saw the Mevlevi Whirling Dervishes perform in, of all places, a hall in the main railway station. A Sufi tradition, frowned on by both Ataturk's secular state and the majority Sunni Muslims, the ceremony is forbidden as a form of worship. It can only be a folkloric dance for tourists (how useful for the Tourist Board). A dozen men and women in big gowns and tall brown felt hats whirled to the music for 40 or 50 minutes, at a constant speed and rhythm. That's all there was to it. No patterns, no choreography. Each was in the process of finding God. It was hypnotic. Nobody fell over or staggered about looking dizzy, and they didn't use the trick that ballerinas do of whipping the head round sharpish so they could concentrate on one spot; they just pivoted on one foot, stretched out their arms, bent their heads to one side and gave a twirl. For nearly an hour. Then at the end they slowly came to a standstill, bowed and retrieved their black cloaks. Without falling over.

I think the brilliant thing is that the Turkish government and the Sufi Muslims have found a workable compromise. The Government believes that the Dervishes are performing for tourists and that's fine. The Dervishes quietly perform their ceremony for real, spinning in time with the universe and continuing the Mevlevi traditional form of worship. As long as the tourists can watch, and both sides keep their own counsel, everybody's happy. Good luck to them.

I'd just like to know how a whirling dervish unwinds at the end of the day.

Gallipoli

We wanted to visit the Gelibolu peninsula, having left it too late to beat our way upwind past it in Yanina, so we took a tour from Istanbul. Gallipoli was only one campaign in the First World War but it was bad enough, and too close to living memory to joke about. It was trench warfare in miniature. Our Turkish guide told us that the trenches were so close together that hand grenades were tossed back and forth three or four times before exploding, and shooting was so intense that bullets collided in the air. The landings were badly botched, particularly in Suvla Bay, where the British commander slept on board ship while his troops struggled ashore, to be decimated by fire from the Turkish soldiers, led by a young Mustafa Kemal. A total of 130,000 died.

Nobody won except Mustafa Kemal, who shot up the political career ladder to become Atatürk - father of modern Turkey.

Troy: from the horse's mouth

Our tour took in Hisarlik, the best bet for the site of ancient Troy, across the water from Gallipoli. Set in flat low-lying land, Troy gained its wealth from controlling the trade route up to Byzantium and the Black Sea. Apart from a 30-foot high wooden horse, which could be a leftover from a movie, the site is not initially that impressive. It's a giant layer cake, consisting of more Troys than you can  shake a Greek at, starting with Troys I to V, covered by VI, VII, VIIa and IX, and topped by a sprinkling of tourists. Nobody knows which layer is the basis for Homer's Iliad and the Hollywood epic but the smart money is on Troy VIIa, mainly because it was seriously demolished by somebody who really didn't like the Trojans.

Carry On Adultering

Here's how it all happened. Helen of Troy, the most beautiful woman in the world, was actually Greek, from Sparta, and she was born from a goose egg (who writes this stuff? Oh yes, that Homer chap). In return for a golden apple, Aphrodite promised her to Paris even though she was already married to Menelaus, King of Sparta, just down the road from Mistra if you remember. While Menelaus was away in Crete at a kick-the-goat's-bladder semi-final, Paris made his move and made his Judgement ('This one's a little cracker. I'll 'ave 'er'), slipped her one without delay, and they ran away together to Troy. Menelaus got back to Sparta after extra time along with all his fellow kick-the-goat's-bladder fans, and they all took off after the elopers.

Thus was Troy flattened. All Aphrodite's fault. Must have been some apple.

Tacking tactics

The flat land around the archaeological site gives you a clue as to why Troy ultimately lost its power and position - silt. You can't be a thriving prosperous port surrounded by acres of mud. But our guide at Hisarlik gave us an interesting additional conjecture, which I'd still like to bottom out, which is that Troy's ultimate decline from being the well-to-do Bristol of the Dardanelles was due to the development of the lateen sail. The lateen couldn't compete with the square-rig when going downwind, but unlike the square-rig it *could* go upwind - it could tack, and that was a first at the time. And whoever the lateen-equipped traders were, Greeks, Arabs, Carthaginians, they didn't get the bus like we did. There *was* no bus, so they tacked all the way into the Dardanelles current up to Byzantium and the Black Sea. Without stopping to pay extortionate harbour fees to anybody.

Who needed Troy now?

Pets on board

Let's have a break from all this history and have a look at our furry friends afloat. Although cats are traditionally easier to look after on the land, we've mainly come across dogs as yacht pets. It probably comes down to toilets again. Cats tend to hide what they do, which could give you a nasty surprise when you snuggle up in your duvet, whereas people seem to be able to train their dogs to achieve miraculous feats of sphincter control. 'Oh, he's very good, he can wait for a couple of days till we get in to port.' Poor mutt.

We met a couple in Malta who had a solution to this problem. They had two large dogs, the slobbery type. The skipper had a ladder on the stern that he could lower into the sea. When the dogs needed to go, they jumped into the sea, did what they had to do, then scrambled up the ladder. Amazing. Would you do that? Maybe if you got a biscuit afterwards. But for most people it's…

Walkies!

And if you're at anchor that means a dinghy ride to shore. But why wear out your outboard just for your dog's convenience? Why not try this?

But you do need a fair-sized dog - or a pair of Jack Russells. Or maybe a couple of dozen Maltese Pocket Dogs. Oh alright, maybe not.

Touline and the pirates

Small dogs are much easier to have on board though. Touline, a Yorkshire terrier who spoke French and English belonged to Penny and Michel. She could fit into a small plastic crate on the back of a bike, or a basket on the front. She didn't shed hairs. Unlike a male dog she didn't pee on the lines or the coachroof. She was trained not to jump, so Penny and Michel always knew where she was, and they could get on with running the boat. She was also trained not to bark, a blessing in a crowded anchorage. In rough weather when it was too unsafe to go on deck Touline would go below. In order to stop

Laces

Rubbery knobbly bits on sole

her from skidding side to side in the saloon, Penny made her some funky non-skid sea boots.

As Penny and Michel were planning to head down the Red Sea I wondered how they and Touline would deal with pirates.

Red Sea pirates were no problem for Nirvana...

107

Cats and other pets

Cats are… well, they're cats aren't they? They're not big slobbering friendly dogs, and you wouldn't get one to jump in the sea, poo and climb out again. No way. But they do look after themselves. And they are really good at eating cockroaches, which can't be a bad thing on a boat.

A parrot on the other hand might well eat roaches but it could be a bit disruptive while it tried to catch them. At least it could give you a running commentary.

Finally, why not just accept the inevitable. Forget the dog, cat and parrot, and have cockroaches as pets. You don't have to get them chipped or tattooed or issue a Pet's Passport. They feed themselves, usually when you're asleep, and they don't need to be taken for walkies. They're ideal! And when you find yourself adrift in the Pacific, they're a valuable source of protein and will help to stave off cannibalism. But only if you can catch them.

Go west old man

It was time to leave Turkey. But before heading west we wanted to explore the coast around Fethiye Bay, Kaş and Kekova, and we're glad we did. Fethiye offers great sailing - steady winds and flat seas. Kekova and the village of Kaleköy are a delight. An elongated island shelters a roadstead with a channel into a totally sheltered bay with excellent holding. Walk up to Kaleköy's miniature Byzantine castle with a village girl as your guide, past women beating carob pods, and look along the promontory to a necropolis of Lycian tombs, huge carved stone houses for the dead, scattered on the hillside stretching down into the water.

An earthquake once drowned not only tombs but a couple of ancient cities. On the other side of an isthmus, all red soil and black goats, you can swim along above an old harbour wall, six or seven feet underwater. Sink down and rub your feet in the silt and you reveal patterned tiles. The ruins spread out of the water and up over a walled hilltop. Climb up there through more tombs and walk the ancient ramparts. It's a magical place, and very hard to leave.

I wish I hadn't told you about it now. You'll go there and tell everyone else.

See you Simi

But we had to go. The Greek islands beckoned and they can be just as beautiful as Turkey. Simi for example. It should really be in Turkey, it's so close, although the Greeks wouldn't thank me for saying so. From Simi we planned to go to Crete, but guess what? We were headed by Westerlies, bang on the nose. We had a re-think, and did big island-hops up through the Cyclades, from Astypalea to Santorini to Milos, aiming for the Corinth Canal as our route into the Ionian.

Santorini

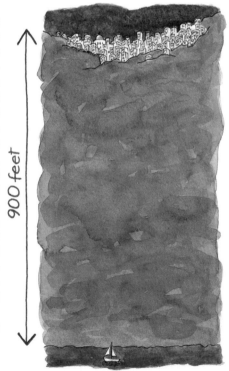

Full of tourists but still a breathtaking sort of place. Sailing through the caldera and looking *up* at the white villages perched on top of the 900-foot high cliffs was a fantastic experience. The sickle-shaped main island and its companion Therasia are all that remain of the rim of a volcano which erupted 3,600 years ago. According to Wikipedia, bless it, the eruption caused the decline of the Minoan civilisation, a tidal wave in Crete, violent rainstorms in Egypt, and a change of dynasty in China, accompanied by a yellow fog, frost in July and withered crops. It was one of the most powerful eruptions ever. It gave rise to the Atlantis legend, and has even been cited as the basis of the Exodus story.

Looks like the Greeks got the blame for everything…

900 feet

What's four miles long and costs 125 euros?

You guessed it. A Corinth Canal trip. But what the heck, it was a great experience and worth it not to have to beat our way west around the Peloponnese. We were followed by a rather large cargo ship but they didn't catch us up. Nobody was bungee jumping from the bridges either, but we enjoyed it all the same.

Once you're through and into the Gulf of Corinth, the weather is anyone's guess. People have been known to duck into Corinth Yacht Harbour to shelter from Force 10 winds. We found dead calm and flat glassy water. Then a breeze ruffled the surface and we could sail, tacking nicely up the gulf. Fun! When did we last do this? The wind stiffened to 30 knots and our tacks got wider and flatter until we were in danger of becoming an unofficial Gulf of Corinth ferry. Engine on again and into the anchorage on the island of Trizonia. The wind blew on for two days, then seemed to drop. We chanced it, and once we rounded the island and reached the open water of the Gulf the wind just keeled over, laid down and died. I shouted at it, kicked it and prodded it with a sharp stick, but nothing doing. To paraphrase the Parrot Sketch this wind was deceased, defunct, dead, no more, an ex-zephyr. It usually happens. I guess after three seasons in the Med we should have remembered. Maybe it's my goldfish bowl memory that's the problem.

Further up the Gulf is Navpaktos, the perfect miniature medieval harbour. With a small yacht you could just squeeze in but it's usually full. The Battle of Lepanto was fought just outside here in 1571. Maybe they were all fighting to get a place in the harbour.

Carry on under the stunning Rio-Antirrio road bridge. Will the mast get under? Won't it? Yes. No. Yes! Phew! With only a few hundred feet to spare. That was a close call.

You can stop at Messolonghi, where Lord Byron popped his clogs after a brief but full life of scribbling, swimming and humping. Apart from that and three Ottoman sieges during the Greek War of Independence, nothing much seems to have happened here for centuries. They do a lot of fishing though.

And these fishermen's stilt houses on the channel leading to the harbour have been here for centuries too. It's a peaceful sort of place. Bit of a backwater, Messolonghi, but the new marina may change all that. I hope not.

Levkas to Malta... to Levkas... to Malta... sod it, back to Levkas

One really nice thing about this way of life is that you can meet complete strangers for a day or maybe only an hour, but you've both got the time to sit and chat, and thus get a fascinating glimpse into the lives of others. We met Tim and Hilary on the harbour wall in Levkas Town. Tim used to deliver yachts, and on one trip took along a spotty seventeen-year-old gas fitter from Huddersfield. Half way across Biscay the weather forced them to turn back for the Solent. In the Hamble River a tall ship was in for a refit, and the boy signed on, heeding Tim's advice to work hard and make himself indispensable. He went round the world on that ship, and then did it again several times on others. He's now married to a half-French, half-Indonesian girl, and has a house in Mallorca. It is on such threads that our lives hang. Would you go back to gas fitting in Huddersfield?

While listening to Tim's story I was packing part of our thirty-year-old Cetrek autopilot in my rucksack, resigned to taking it to Luigi the Pirate, as he is known locally, who was going to charge me an arm and a leg or two to try and fix it. 'Go and talk to him but don't leave anything with him to repair,' someone had said. I had one foot on our plank when I asked Tim if he knew any local electronics experts. 'Yes I do. A German who speaks perfect English and knows his stuff. Here's his number.' I removed my foot from the plank and went below to look for my mobile. On boats you learn so much from just chatting to people.

Our Cetrek autopilot was built like a tank. A WW11 tank. A week and a half before talking to Tim, it had started to go a little senile and would occasionally turn us in ever decreasing circles, always to port, until we were in danger of disappearing up our own stern gland. Not much use on a three-day trip to Malta then. So I had faced a day or so on the harbour wall while I repaired it. Piece of cake. Got the manual out and read it. Took the lid off the big round thingummy that has a knob on its bottom that you twist to change course. I was amazed. It was a miracle of 1970s opto-electronics, looking like something from Wallace and Gromit's garage. I fiddled around a bit, cleaned it (worth a try when you don't know what you're doing), read a bit more, then discovered that there were two other boxes of electronics that I could fiddle with. Oh joy...

By the end of Day Two, I needed help. I'd been to see Luigi the Pirate in his shop, and picked his brains as much as I could without getting to the point where I might have to pay him anything.

'Do you know of anyone who knows about repairing these things?' I asked him. 'The only man I can think of died about ten years ago. We'd need a séance to get in touch with him,' he said drily, thinking: I bet I could charge him a packet to hold a séance. 'Bring it in and I'll have a look at it.' 'OK,' I replied, thinking: I bet he'd try and charge me a packet to hold a séance.

We retreated for a rethink. Somebody told me about an electrician who worked on boats. Within an hour of my call a battered little van turned up, disgorging a cheerful Frenchman with a bag of tools. This was Olivier. Olivier was from the Ardèche. He'd taken a year out to go to Greece, and then decided not to go back to the rat race. Now 48, he lived on a boat in the next harbour, but returned to France every winter.

'To avoid the winter rain here?' I asked. 'Non, I go back for the culture. There's nothing here. No cinema, no theatre, no galleries.' He did drawings in line and watercolour of old local houses and sold them in Edith's shop in the town. We decided to stop jawing and get down to it. I lifted the lid on what I now knew to be the compass.

'Ha!' said Olivier. 'Military spec. A modern autopilot wouldn't last thirty years - more like five, then you throw it away. Absolute merde. See these two things? They are light sensors.' 'Ah! I wondered when you'd spot that,' I said. His meter showed the resistance across one to be 100 times less than the other. He swapped them, and the needle moved the other way. It was a eureka moment. Olivier removed them, each with its tiny disc of polarising film, and promised to order similar ones from France on the internet. They could be delivered just in time to a French friend who would soon be in Greece. Fantastic! Result!

Five days later, Olivier's friend was in Greece. The parts were in a Post Office somewhere in the Ardèche. Olivier's friend was desolé, as only the French can be. Olivier was desolé. As he handed my old sensors back to me, he was even more desolé, because he'd lost one of the precious polarising filters. I too was now desolé. We went to look for it on the floor of his van. The van also was desolé, and would, I'm sure, have given a Gallic shrug had the engine been running. So, square one to square one in ten days.

But what the heck, this is boat maintenance, right? Just get on with it. The internet café came to my rescue. The identical sensors were miraculously still made after 30 years and I found a website with some polarising filter material. All I had to do was get the scissors and a soldering iron and we'd be in business.

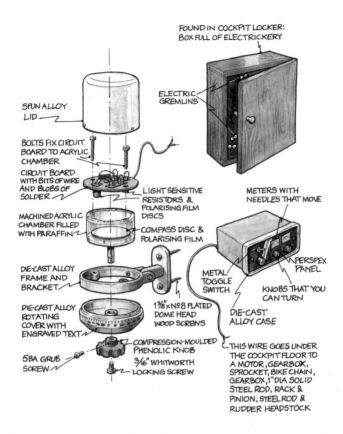

FOUND IN COCKPIT LOCKER:
BOX FULL OF ELECTRICKERY

SPUN ALLOY LID

ELECTRIC GREMLINS

BOLTS FIX CIRCUIT BOARD TO ACRYLIC CHAMBER

CIRCUIT BOARD WITH BITS OF WIRE AND BLOBS OF SOLDER

LIGHT SENSITIVE RESISTORS & POLARISING FILM DISCS

METERS WITH NEEDLES THAT MOVE

MACHINED ACRYLIC CHAMBER FILLED WITH PARAFFIN

COMPASS DISC & POLARISING FILM

DIE-CAST ALLOY FRAME AND BRACKET

METAL TOGGLE SWITCH

PERSPEX PANEL

KNOBS THAT YOU CAN TURN

DIE-CAST ALLOY ROTATING COVER WITH ENGRAVED TEXT

1⅜" × №8 PLATED DOME HEAD WOOD SCREWS

DIE-CAST ALLOY CASE

5BA GRUB SCREW

COMPRESSION-MOULDED PHENOLIC KNOB

3/16" WHITWORTH LOCKING SCREW

THIS WIRE GOES UNDER THE COCKPIT FLOOR TO A MOTOR, GEARBOX, SPROCKET, BIKE CHAIN, GEARBOX, 1"DIA SOLID STEEL ROD, RACK & PINION, STEEL ROD & RUDDER HEADSTOCK

I cut the discs, glued them in, soldered the sensors, put it all back together and we went for a test sail. Engine on, dead ahead, engage autopilot.

We went round in a circle. Oh shit. Back on the harbour wall then. At this point we met Tim and Hilary, and found our German electronics man. He came on board. We took all the lids off, switched everything on, and ignoring his fancy expensive testing equipment, he closed his eyes and just touched all the bits with his fingers, literally a laying on of hands. 'Dis here is a liddle varm. I sink dis is der problem.' I caught Liz's eye. What kind of unearthly force were we dealing with here? I shrugged (having caught the habit from Olivier). At this point I decided I had to have faith. We ordered new parts, which by a miracle arrived a couple of days later. 'Twas then that a still small voice spake unto me and told me we should be not in doubt, and just nip out again for a test sail before fitting them.

And lo! Verily did the autopilot guide us in a straight line through the troubled waters of the deep, just outside Levkas harbour. And for sooth the Holy Auto-relic hath been without sin ever since, yea even across the mighty Atlantic.

I can only put it down to the proximity of Malta and St Paul's Wristbone.

Summer in Malta

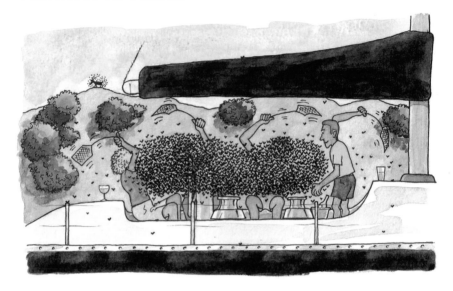

We got to Malta in the end. It was the height of summer, hot as a very hot thing, and all of Libya's flies had come over to the islands for their holidays. We met our friends Roger and Lisa on Kimo Sabe and spent a languid and enjoyable yet energetic afternoon drinking, chatting and despatching about five million of them to that great cowpat in the sky.

Our Cetrek Mk II Auto-relic, homing in on the Holy Wristbone, had led us to St Paul's Bay where we met my nephew's family. We anchored in front of their hotel balcony, and took them on the boat for the first time. Young Fred's main interest was fishing from the dinghy, but as fish hooks and inflatables don't really mix well, we took them off on a sail to an anchorage for lunch, not knowing how they'd like the boat's motion.

Five-year-old Robert wasn't too sure at first, but as soon as we picked up a breeze and Yanina heeled over and dipped her gunwales in the sea, he was laughing like a drain. In fact they all were. Maybe we'll leave them the boat when we've done with it.

But not just yet...

The End

Where did we come from? What are we? Where are we going? What did we spend it all on?

So Paul Gauguin asked in his finest painting and I don't think he ever got an answer. To avoid having to pose these existential questions we decided to print our own banknotes illustrating our route. That way we'd know exactly where we were and at least we'd have made some money along the way.

At present the exchange rate between the Yannie and the rest of the world's currencies is not that great and if I were you I would wait for a while before you cut these notes out and spend them.

The next book
A hippo on the nose

Malta was a stepping stone, but then so is everywhere you go on a boat. You find a place, get to know it, get bored with it and move on. As a friend put it, 'When the barman knows your name it's time to go.'

We were heading for Tunisia. Yes, the place where we thought we'd spend our first liveaboard winter three years and one book ago. So much for planning. We didn't stay long there but we made the most of it. And familiar as it is to many people, it's *Africa*. A different continent and a different culture. And a different approach to food hygiene, but let's not spoil the mood, I'm getting quite lyrical here.

And Tunisia itself was another stepping stone. Lemming-like, we just carried on west, back to Spain again, then Gibraltar, down the Atlantic coast of Morocco to the Canaries. Here we met a bunch of French sailors who were going to Senegal. Blimey, that's a bit brave isn't it? Should we join them? In the end only we went, and Senegal and the Gambia River, where we met our hippos, our crocodiles and other interesting characters, were a revelation as only West Africa can be.

You can read all about it in *A hippo on the nose*.

So where did we go from there? Well, the world was our bearded bivalve that goes so well with a pint of Guinness. Cape Verdes? Caribbean? Brazil? It's all out there. Once you escape the Med…

Prize draw winner

From the thousands of bookmarks which we handed out to people at the Boat Shows, and which went to bookshops and chandleries, we pulled Ted Holmes' name out of the peaked cap as winner of the draw and you can see him on page 66. A copy of *Bang on the nose* goes to Ted.

Reference

Adams, Douglas, *Hitchhiker's Guide to the Galaxy*, published by Pan, 1979

Bradford, Ernle, *The Great Siege: Malta 1565*, published by Penguin, 1964

Fermor, Patrick Leigh, *Mani: Travels in the Southern Peloponnese*, Penguin, 1984

Heikell, Rod, *Greek Waters Pilot*, published by Imray, 2007

Heikell, Rod, *Mediterranean Cruising Handbook,* published by Imray, 2004

Thanks to *Wikipedia*, for checking all my half-remembered facts and giving me half-reliable answers.

Painting of Helen and Paris by Jacques-Louis David

Competition winner

In *On the nose* there was a cartoon called *Ice cream in Stintino*, in which I couldn't for the life of me think of how to fill the speech bubble and I asked for suggestions. Here's what Kay and Peter on Wild Thyme suggested. My thanks and a free copy of *Bang on the nose* goes to them.

With a little help from my friends

'What is your position?' 'I'm standing by the fridge.' VHF joke from Gary who taught us Mediterranean mooring and much, much more.

Thanks to Keith and Jean Nicholson on La Liberté for John Masefield's poem:
A very queer thing is the wind, I don't know how it beginn'd
And nobody knows where it goes, It is wind, it beginn'd, and it blows.

Thanks to Mike Darling for providing the time and space, Andrew Morley, Lynne McPeake, Rod Heikell, Jenny Darling, Nicky Clarke, Michael Shaw, Audrey, Ian and Sue, Nige and Al, Penny and Michel, Terry Smallwood, Mike Kerr, and everybody else who wrote and told me how much they enjoyed *On the nose*.

And most of all, Liz. Thank you for your support. I'm still wearing it since the last book.